Just Kids

Just Kids

How to Survive the Twos to Twelves

Michael Rosen

Illustrations by Caroline Holden

JOHN MURRAY
Albemarle Street, London

Text © Michael Rosen 1995

Illustrations © Caroline Holden 1995

First published in 1995
by John Murray (Publishers) Ltd.,
50 Albemarle Street, London W1X 4BD

A catalogue record for this book is available from the British Library

ISBN 0-7195-5680-5

Typeset in 11 on 13 Palatino by Servis Filmsetting Ltd.
Printed and bound in Great Britain by The University Press, Cambridge

Contents

Introduction

Some evenings my wife and I remind each other that we have just spent the previous three hours talking about one or other of our children. She or I might make a casual passing comment about one of them: 'she's looking very tired, isn't she?' and this leads into a chat about how tiredness shows on her face more than the others, which then leads into what she was like when she was a baby and how she's coping with the new school and – whoosh – the three hours have gone.

We're not the only parents in the world doing this, there are millions of us at it, sitting up till the wee hours yacking away about what's going wrong and what's going right. The bald contemplation of this, the hours spent, the energy used up, can sometimes puzzle me, but perhaps it shouldn't. After all, we're involved in an intimate engagement with several small human beings whom we have known in one way or another from their first little wriggle or kick in the womb. One of the reasons we keep talking about it is because it keeps changing. The moment you try to analyse what is going on with them, something changes – a cat dies, a new best-friend appears, the bed becomes too small. Even minor change can, at first, appear mysterious and unsettling so the first thing we need to do about it is talk. What's happening? Why's it happening? What can we do about it?

This book is meant to be a contribution to that conversation. It isn't a manual or a complete top-to-toe guide on how to bring up children. It is the out-loud thoughts of someone who has been in the thick of bringing up five of them. I had two boys with my first wife, with whom I did 50-50 share of the care, though she might put the figure at 60-40, with her taking the heavier load. My second wife had two girls before we married and, as I say to children in schools when they ask, 'we did one together – which makes five.' I see the first two boys half the week, the girls are with us virtually all the time and the last chap literally all the time. In my second marriage I've done much less than 50-50 or even 60-40, which also provides us with much to discuss and talk about until the wee hours.

What is said here is born very much out of my own experiences, some of which are fairly characteristic of British middle-class life but others, because of my peculiar working life as a freelance writer, broadcaster and performer, are less typical. This will explain the fact, for example, that unlike many other professionals we have managed largely to get through life without hiring in help. Hence the book doesn't deal with nannies and au pairs. There may be other glaring omissions apparent to people without my prejudices and bias but before you gnash your teeth might I say that this book is intended to be no more than a way of opening a conversation. If at times I sound as if I am laying down the law, then this is a personality fault of mine and need not be taken as some kind of instruction. Please treat this book as one side in a discussion, a position with which you can argue or which you can simply reject. If in flicking through the pages you also find yourself smiling, even if it is with that knowing, ironic shrug that is familiar to all parents trying to cope, then I shall be delighted.

I should also say that it is a kind of sequel. No, this is not *Childrearing II*, but a follow-up to *Goodies and Daddies: An A–Z Guide to Fatherhood* which dealt with what it's like to be a father of babies and toddlers. It was my editors, Caroline Knox and Kate Chenevix Trench, who coaxed and wheedled this book out of me. They now point out that my children are still growing and soon they will all have been teenagers, and as Arnie and Sigourney have done sequels to sequels, why not you, Michael? In the meantime, I hope this one offers up something to chew on.

Bedtime

You could quite easily make an argument that western civilization depends on bedtime. Or rather, that if we slept in say, two or three stretches in 24 hours western civilization would collapse. I guess it's why, when teenagers start doing just that, everyone gets anxious. So we keep saying to ourselves: we must teach children good habits; they must have at least ten hours sleep; they must have deep sleep – and so on. What we really mean is that if you, little children, are going to fit into the routines of the western world – GO TO BED!!! There is also a sub-plot: all parents remember ancient times, B.C. (Before Children). Those were the days when time drifted by listening to records, slipping out to an Italian restaurant, having a spur-of-the-moment whim to get into the local before closing time, a late-night movie, a late-night jazz club, a late night. But now, it's not like that. Spontaneous rushings out of the door are not on and increasingly you find that if you try to do anything interesting between eight and ten o'clock at night, children seem to think that they are entitled to have some of it too.

'Anything interesting' can cover literally anything: TV news, a conversation with your spouse, painting the skirting board, scratching your head. It seems that just as children get to the point where their bodies should be getting sluggish, the concentration span coming down to 0.0001 secs, instead they start getting energy surges. If you're talking about earthquakes in Japan, they suddenly want to know all about the Richter Scale. If you've decided to cut your toenails, suddenly they're on hand to offer to cut the little toenail for you. They might suddenly find that you need hugging – for half an hour. The wrong kind of biscuits was opened at tea-time and so several minutes must be spent looking for the right kind, the ones you definitely bought at the weekend but are now right at the back of the cupboard. Bedtime is delay time.

Some parents that I know think that all this is fine. They say that if we have children, they are part of our lives so why expel them at eight or nine o'clock at night? Let them just hang out with us and that will be the best education they'll ever have. If they're tired the next day, it doesn't matter much because they'll go to bed earlier the next night to catch up. Then there are others who say, 'We try to get them to go to bed but they just won't go. When we put them to bed, they just jump up again like jack-in-the-boxes.' In other words children's bedtimes are really about adult space. If you think that adults don't need their own space and children should be able to hang about with adults if they want to, then bedtime is no big deal. It might drive your friends completely crazy: they thought they were coming over for a chat about the council's granting of planning permission for a nuclear waste dump at the end of your garden and instead they find themselves having a conversation about Lego. But you tell them that the 'marvellous thing about Italians is that their children just know when to go to bed and don't feel cut out of their parents' lives. We saw it in Tuscany this summer and . . .'

For parents who would dearly love their children to be out of sight by nine but are still arguing with them at twelve, then life can be hell. Every evening becomes a battleground. The children know that you want them out of the way, they realize that you're not strong enough to manage it, so this makes them, in effect, more anxious and less willing to head off into the dark place called Bedroom. They might be thinking: 'Why should we trust you to look after us when we shut our eyes in the dark when you are weaker than us when it comes to getting us to do what you want?' It's a perfect vicious circle: the less successful you are in getting them to bed, the more anxious and hyperactive they become, the less successful you become and so on. It's even worse when parents have a different view on the matter. Mum wants the kids in bed on the dot but Dad has only just got in and says they can stay up longer. The kids work the lever in the gap and start wheedling. Or Dad says he wants to watch the TV without the kids walking in and out and Mum reminds him that this is the only time in his life when he will have children of this age and he'll live to regret it. Meanwhile the kids hang about in doorways, snuffling. Bedtimes are really an expression of the personalities of parents.

If you feel you've lost control and would like to get your children to bed earlier, then some of the following may be of help:

● bring in a routine eg. bath, milk and biscuits, story. Try and stick to it for at least five nights a week.
● have time deadlines so that if the child breaks them then something pleasurable is lost eg. the right to stay up late on Friday night to watch a favourite TV programme.
● there obviously can and should be exceptions to the routine but these must have agreed limits eg. you must have had your bath and be in pyjamas before the programme begins. If you hang about after the programme you lose the right to watch it next week.
● even if you can't make a child sleep, you can reach an agreement that they should be in their room, settling down, by a certain time.

● if it's possible, make sure that bedtimes are pleasurable – or at the very least, not unpleasant. Sharing books, stories, games and general chat are the easiest ways. Books have the advantage of being of a fixed length and/or in chapters.

It is worth bearing in mind that for very young children bedtime is horrible because they're being separated from you. It's like saying goodbye to you, going away into a separate place, away from cuddles and fun. It's a place where if you wake up in the middle of the night, it will be dark, your parents will be miles away, inert, and if they wake up, grumpy. In fact the whole thing is not only nasty but when it comes down to it, also fairly pointless and unnecessary. As we don't live like our ancestors who let children run around till they dropped and then shipped them into bed alongside us, then bedtime is basically a con. We are conning our little children that going to their bedrooms is just as exciting and nice as sitting on us in a warm, bright sitting-room. We're conning them that getting into bed and shutting their eyes is a really brilliant thing to do. They also have the suspicion that when they close their eyes, you might die, run away or disappear, demons might come and grab them, or large spiders who live under their beds will come out and sit on their faces. In short whatever we do at bedtime with very small children, it'd better be very nice, very reassuring, very calming and after all that it may not work anyway.

Some people say that it is utterly wrong to sit with your very young children as they go to sleep because if they wake up in the night they won't have the psychological and emotional resources to cope with being alone in a bed. Others say that by sitting with children till they doze off gives them reassurance and this enables them to cope better with fears and worries. Yer takes yer pick. Most people, myself included, try a mix of both. When they were going through something difficult, like a parental separation or first day at school, then I'd sit with them but at other times I chose not to. Of course that leaves you open to all kinds of manipulation and, albeit unconsciously, children may be quite keen to split Mum and Dad up for an hour or so in order to take a lion's share of attention for themselves. You might think that you're doing some reassuring when in actual fact you are just a stooge sitting there being monopolized. Can small children really be like that? You bet they can.

Bedwetting

The last time I wet the bed was when I was about ten and very pleasurable it was too. I can remember that it involved a dream about being on holiday and not being able to get back to the campsite in time. So I just stopped behind a tree and had a pee. Except I wasn't standing behind a tree, I was in bed. It is difficult to sort out whether this was linked to anxiety – which child psychologists tend to believe – or whether I was having a dream that just happened to involve a pee. What seems most likely, is that I was having an anxiety dream that transferred my worries about passing the 11-plus examination on to another worry about campsites – and having a pee was a release from this. Until I woke up.

It always seems to me amazing that we can not only learn how to control peeing when we are conscious but also when we are asleep. After all, it is worth remembering that virtually all the apparatus that controls peeing is 'involuntary', that is to say under the control of the part of the nervous system that is responsible for such things as digestion, pupil dilation and hearing. It is literally only the last centimetre or so that is under our conscious control. Somewhere between the ages of twelve months and three years our babes mostly get the hang of this when they're awake. In essence they discover that incredible centimetre and learn how to make it stop or release the flow. (To find out how good you are at it as an adult try this: go to the loo, start peeing and see if you can stop the flow mid-stream. This is not simply a private trick. If you have a child who is, say, older than five or six and is regularly wetting the bed, learning this trick may help them with night-time control. It's funny as well.)

So how do we learn to avoid wetting the bed at night? Well, clearly the brain develops a circuit that can guard the door even when the rest of the brain has gone to sleep. Except when we're, say, anxious or ill and the guard is swept aside – or is it hood-winked?

First rule for parents is that we mustn't load the child with yet another layer of anxiety by getting all het up about the bedwetting itself. A plastic cover that goes on the mattress under the sheets is a vital accessory – don't forget that your occasional bed-wetting child will need it on holiday, for sleep-overs and other visits with friends and relations. The morning bath and/or shower with plenty of soap is also an essential otherwise the child will smell of pee. Try not to make this seem either like a punish-ment or a reward – in the old days the bath used to be cold and the odd whack across the bare bum was thought to be very useful. On the other hand it might be that the bedwetting is about grabbing your attention, worrying over whether they're getting enough affection and so a nice warm bath with lots of cuddling might be what they wanted in the first place. Better to provide that at bed-time, rather than giving it as a reward for bedwetting.

Some parents, it has to be said, are over-ambitious for their chil-dren, and expect them to be dry at night too early, or expect that when a child is dry it should always be dry. There are plenty of children (two out of my five), who weren't completely dry at night until they were seven. If it is anxiety that causes this, then it has to be said that in the spectrum of human responses to anxiety, it is surely one of the least anti-social and considerably less unpleasant or worrying than, say, bullying, spitefulness, and eat-ing disorders.

Useful aids to avoiding bedwetting – and remember it is the child you are helping, not yourself – are a potty under the bed, a lit passageway from the bed to the toilet and a light on all night in the toilet, a pee last thing at night, sharing famous bed-wetting stories from your past and having fun with the stop-the-flow exercises I described earlier. All this cuts down on shame – a truly corrosive feeling to have here.

Now for the deep question: what might your child be anxious about? Something going on at school? Rows between parents? A death? Over-ambitious demands either from school, you, or friends? Or maybe you have a child who is generally a bit strung out about things. All this needs time and talk. It took us ages to find out that one of our children was getting very anxious about how, or if, he could get into the in crowd that played football (*see also* FRIENDS). It seems as if part of being anxious about something is being unable or unwilling to talk about it. All our wit and empathy have to be on hand to help a child to bring worries to the surface and talk about them. And for that to happen, they must also feel totally safe.

With both the physical aids and the emotional help it may be that a bedwetting child will stop. On the other hand the child may not. If you are really worried and it's going on after the age of, say, eight, then a visit to a GP – one who is used to dealing with children in a sympathetic way – might be in order.

Bullies

I am sadly over-qualified to talk about this. I was a bully. I can think of at least half a dozen people who, nearly forty years or so later, must regularly curse my name. There were kids whom I picked on for being fat, or weak, or toothy, or smooth. I usually used verbal mockery, picking on mannerisms and using nicknames. I would get a crowd on my side to join in and laugh so that the person would feel defenceless. It's a grisly story that embarrasses me even now. Quite why I needed to do this is not totally clear to me. I was the youngest in the family and perhaps (though not consciously) felt that I was the weakest and so needed to bump myself up when I got away from them. I was a bit over-protected by my mother and perhaps it was a way of proving that I wasn't really a mummy's boy and could be tough if I wanted to. Whatever the reason, here was I, a product of a two-up, two-down nuclear family with no apparent trauma in sight, who wreaked havoc in playgrounds for several years and made various totally unexceptional, unobnoxious kids' lives a complete misery for weeks on end.

I say this, not only to get it off my chest but also to point out two things: your own dearest who kisses you goodbye at the school gate and appears to be largely without cares or worries may in fact be as revolting a bully as I was. Or conversely, your own dearest who kisses you goodbye at the school gate and appears to be largely without cares or worries may in fact be on the receiving end of a revolting bully like me. Out there on the playground children are discovering who has power and who hasn't and it's a serious business.

The most dangerous thing about bullying is that it works. It makes the bully feel better for a while, he (or she) can quickly see the effect. I remember – to my shame – the satisfaction I got from seeing my victim try to get away from me, flinch, cry, complain or whatever. It was my fix. As I write this, I am trying to think of ways in which my position could have been or was broken down. One boy, Richard Russell, whom I had picked on for wearing Brylcreem and being rather well organized with his pens and pencils, got more and more frustrated with my mockery. In the end he came to school one day, tapped me on the shoulder and when I turned to face him, slapped my face and said very loudly so everyone could hear, 'My Dad taught me that.' I seem to remember he had one or two other tricks like that and they worked. I lay off him. Clearly, his Dad was on to something. He didn't come to the school and complain that I was calling his son silly names, as that would have made it worse for the boy. Instead he armed his son with a strategy that made me look foolish while at the same time it announced the possible intervention of larger forces if the need arose. It didn't cure me of bullying but it cured me of bullying Richard Russell.

There's a lesson there but some snags too. If it's your kid who's the victim, he or she may not be as self-assured as Richard Russell was to take me on physically and verbally at the same time. Plenty of victims don't want any physical or verbal confrontation at all. They just want to be left alone and they are entitled to that. Making such children 'stand up to him' or 'let him have it' may in fact make matters much worse because the child knows that the parent is asking for the impossible. The other snag is if it's your child who is the bully he hasn't been cured.

As bullying is about power, then the only way to break bullying is to break the grip of power. This is done in American movies and old public school stories with someone bullying the bully so that he is either shamed, smashed or killed and we all go home feeling better in the knowledge that force beats force. Unfortunately, as we also know, this usually solves nothing because the new force in town is just as likely to be a bully as the old one. To break the power of bullies needs intervention by adults in a very particular way. Basically, the bully has to be confronted by victims and sidekicks at the same time. The victims have to be given time and support to tell their stories and name names so that the bully's sidekicks can be shamed up and given a chance to peel off from the bully. The bully has to be asked to articulate what he has done, say it out loud in front of everyone, including, ideally, his parents. He has to make a contract with everyone present that it won't happen again.

Sadly, this procedure doesn't often take place and the whole matter is usually dealt with behind closed doors by headteachers and maybe one set of parents at a time. All this does is reinforce the power of the bully who is in essence flattered by the attention from the chief guy around, the headteacher. It doesn't break the hold that the bully has over his sidekicks and it doesn't mean he is faced down by the collective power of the victims. He can return to the classroom with his status intact.

As parents of victims or bullies we can ask teachers to convene meetings like this to have these matters out. Some secondary schools are beginning a pupil-led bullying counselling service. This too strikes me as a good move, enabling victims to get strength and support from each other and neutral observers, but it probably needs support from teachers and parents too.

When I look at these new initiatives I find myself wishing that I had been pulled up and dealt with at the time by teachers, parents, victims and sidekicks. Bullying wasn't taken very seriously at the time and I can remember only fifteen years ago working at a boys' school in London where one of the teacher's ways of dealing with it beggars belief. Young Jason, who prided himself on being able to beat up any other kid in his year, came to the PE teacher on one occasion and said that there was a bit of a rumble going on down by the gym. So the PE teacher said to the boy, 'Well you go and sort it out, will you Jason? After all, you can look after yourself, can't you?' Jason went off, bursting with pride that his position as class bully, class tough guy, was being reinforced and supported by the staff tough guy. Machismo breeds machismo. Hopefully, such approaches are on the way out but it's still easy to find places where bullying isn't taken seriously enough. The best way round that is to share the problem with other parents involved.

Finding out what is happening in children's lives and minds is about the hardest thing I have ever tried to do. The moment they sense that you are trying to find something out is often the cue for them to say absolutely nothing, to lower their eyes and start looking like they're going to be sick. Saying things like, 'I'm only doing this for your own good' or 'I'm doing this to help you, you

know', don't often deliver the goods. Sometimes we only find out what is really going on by getting down to some solid, straight-down-the-middle spying. Of course this is a violation of privacy and it isn't justified in all circumstances at all times. But if you are beginning to fear that something awful is going on and your child is reluctant to talk then, yes, it is under-cover time. In the short term it may well save months of anxiety and terror for you and your children; in the long term it may be the proof (for which children are always asking us in obscure and weird ways) that we are desperately concerned with their safety.

Your job here may be to find out from school, friends or relations whether they know of any bullying going on. If this turns out to be the case, then you have to keep talking about it with your child, share some stories about things that happened to you, friends or relations. Involve the school (if that's where it started), parents of other children who are on the receiving end and, ideally, the parents of the bully. When and if the school says that they are going to deal with it, then it is far better that this doesn't go on either as something secret between the headteacher and the bully's parents nor as simply a very general statement made in assembly that bullying is going on and 'it's high time it stopped.' You are entitled to a more open forum to discuss it in, for the simple reason that bullying thrives on being a furtive out-of-sight sort of thing. If you think the situation requires a meeting between, say, you, your child, any other children on the receiving end and their parents, the relevant teacher, the bully's parents and the bully, then you should ask for it.

The media is full of stories of schools who have not taken bullying seriously. One wonders whether this is another opportunity to play on parents' fears and present schools as dire, blackboard jungles. However, it is true that we don't always get co-operation on bullying from schools, if only because sometimes schools see it as proof that Charles Darwin was writing about children – it sorts out the men from the boys . . . and all that. If you think your child isn't getting the protection that he or she needs in school and life is becoming a misery then you shouldn't have any hesitation about pulling the child out of the school, finding another or, if it really comes down to it, keeping your child at home.

Choosing a Secondary School

'Have you heard? They say the High School is going down the pan.'

'Yes, I've seen the kids on the buses.'

'Where are you thinking of sending Kate?'

'We've had a look at St Mary's.'

'But that's a church school, isn't it? I heard that if you were a Band 1 child you had to prove that you were a Christian.'

'We could do that, I think.'

'Is it any good?'

'Well, that's the thing – I'm not sure it is. The really able girls are going to Broadchester. It's making great strides since it went GM.'

'GM?'

'Grant Maintained. It gets a good slice more of loot, since it came directly under government control.'

'But it's an all-girls' school, isn't it?'

'Yes, I know it's against my principles, and Kate says that she'd prefer a mixed school, but their GCSE results are superb.'

'But isn't that because it's selective?'

'Oh no, they don't select.'

'Well, how do you get in?'

'You kind of write a letter and then if they like that you go for a sort of interview thing. And then if it's looking good there's a sort of quick little test thingy. But that's nothing like the old 11-plus and selection, is it?'

'Isn't it?'

'Where's Sam going?'

'We don't have a choice really, where we're living. It's too far to get him into Yarborough, we're not Christians so he can't go to St

13

Nicholas, the boys' school is GM and I don't think Sam would get through the interview and test thingy, as you put it. So that only leaves the High.'

'Oh God. Really? Have you thought about going private?'

And so it goes on: conversations like this are occurring all over the country as children get to Year 6 (10 and 11 years old). First of all, a quick run down of the different kinds of secondary schools. I do this because it is quite possible that no one will have been straight with you. In your area there may be a range of different kinds of secondary schools.

Mixed comprehensive: funded by the local council, which admits pupils in the following order of priority: siblings of children already at the school, children who live in the catchment area, children who go to feeder primary schools but outside the catchment area and, finally, anyone else. *But* – if it is a popular school, the catchment area gets smaller and smaller and people get more and more desperate to get their kid into the school. So what happens is that people start lying about their addresses. It is known that some headteachers are turning a blind eye to this. In other words popular comprehensives are becoming selective schools by the back door.

Single-sex comprehensive: same as above, and just as likely, if not more so, to be operating a secret selective system.

Grant Maintained: unlike the two above, these schools are funded directly from central government. The parents and teachers, at some time in the last few years, voted to 'opt out' of local government control, and opted into more money and direct control from central government. Quite often such schools are 'old foundation' schools that were forced to go comprehensive in the 1970s and are now finding their way back to being 'grammar schools'. These schools will use some method or other to select their intake. In the past, these have been secretive: nods, winks, children of ex-pupils, letters from parents. They are now under pressure to be more open about it and are using methods such as 'primary school performance' i.e. SATs (Standard Assessment Tasks) and teachers' reports, a test, an informal oral exam and so on. These schools are becoming like the old grammar schools created by the 1944 Education Act, i.e. state schools where entry was dependent on you passing the 11-plus. There are already signs that they are becoming better equipped, attracting more qualified staff and, very importantly, operating a strict exclusion system (expulsions of naughty kids). Because they are not under local control they can exclude children much more easily. And do.

Religious schools: these may or may not be grant maintained, voluntary controlled or voluntary aided. A voluntary aided school (most common at the secondary level) are schools where the building and the capital expenditure is the responsibility of the church or synagogue but the teachers' salaries are paid for out of the public purse. A voluntary controlled school is where the whole establishment is paid for out of the public purse but the church has a place on the board of governors and so determines, to an extent, the Christian input into the school. If these two kinds of schools are also grant maintained then they can openly operate a selective system. If they are not, they will almost certainly be operating a semi-covert one depending on whether parents are regular churchgoers, whether children have been baptized, confirmed, circumcized, bar mitzvahed. (Not all at the same time though!) How come then, people say, there are Muslim children at a Catholic girls' school? Because, *in certain cases*, the governors waive the denominational demands. What cases? Er, this is not always clear other than that there might not be enough Catholic kids in the area but there are plenty of Muslims.

State-assisted places at private schools (*see below*): these are totally dependent on your child passing an entrance exam set by the school.

Independent schools: private, fee-paying schools that are often eighteenth-century (or earlier) foundations. They are usually day schools, and usually, but not always, single-sex. Most of them have an entrance exam that may or may not determine entry. Most of their intake stay on until the sixth form. Most go to university.

Public schools: this usually refers to private boarding schools with high prestige: Rugby, Harrow, Eton. Most of them require you to have put your child down for them when they were very young.

Private 'progressive' schools: various schools make a different pitch, offering care for children with 'problems' or a heavily arts-

based curriculum, a 'personal' system of education based per-
haps on Quaker principles or another educational philosophy.
There are some famous examples: Summerhill, Dartington, St
Christopher's, King Alfred's, Gordonstoun and so on.

Home tuition and off-site education: in a few exceptional cases,
local authorities provide facilities for persistent school refusers,
invalids and semi-delinquents.

'Special' schools: for children with disabilities.

'Education Otherwise': where you or your friends prove to the
local authority that you can educate your children at home. There
is an association and network of parents who support each other
and give advice on how to deal with the law.

'Community Schools': this may mean two quite different things:
i) a community in an area set up a private school. It may well follow a curriculum that matches another country's. In the case of
non-English-speaking schools, naturally, the medium of instruction will mostly be in that language. Most of the children and
teachers are bilingual.

ii) Comprehensive schools under local government control that
are trying to provide facilities, education and a presence in the
locality to suit all ages in the 'community'. This might mean not
much more than evening classes going on in the school or it might
mean that adults can attend daytime all-age school classes, that
adult classes go on all the time on the same site, or any combination of these. I'm someone who thinks this is the rational way
forward for schools – it breaks down the age barriers and
confrontations of secondary schools, it opens up possibilities of
lifetime education for adults, and it provides a cultural and recre-
ational focus for a locality.

Middle Schools: some areas operate a system of first, middle and
'high' schools split into Years 1–4, 5–8, 9–11. In itself it is neither a
good nor a bad thing. Year 8s at some middle schools at least have
the benefit of being top dogs whereas at secondaries they're
usually straining at the leash to be bigger than they are and are
getting sat on because they're not. Where this system still oper-
ates it's mostly non-selective.

Sixth-Form Colleges: more and more areas now provide these
colleges for 16-pluses to do their A-levels, GCSE retakes, Btecs,
GNVQs and other vocational qualifications. In choosing a

secondary school for your 11 year old you may be interested to know what the links are between the school and the local sixth-form college, a 'consortium' and a 'community college' or 'college of further education'. You might be interested to find out whether the teachers teaching your child will also be teaching sixth formers. Some teachers feel that this is the way they can get true job satisfaction, seeing children all the way through.

'Consortia': schools gang together to provide a sixth-form education on several sites, using the teachers from a group of schools. This mixes single-sex schools and gives teachers a chance to teach across a wider range of ages and curricula.

Community Colleges and Colleges of Further Education: these offer an enormous range of courses to almost anyone over the age of 16 who's interested. As secondary school life is only five years, it is often the case that these years don't coincide with the interests, energy and attention of our kids. Though this causes us great worry and concern, all is not lost. These kinds of colleges give kids new chances to find something they might want to do, they make fewer demands on having to be part of a school ethos, classes tend to be made up of people who want to get hold of some more qualifications. Two of my kids are at these and in their own way compensating for the ways in which schooling between eleven and sixteen didn't suit them. In other words, although choosing a school at eleven is of course very important, it is not the final throw of the dice. There are other chances to get a bite of the education cherry at later stages.

City Technical Colleges: in a few big towns and cities, there are government-controlled schools that offer a high-tech curriculum. They are jointly financed by private business and select their pupils on the basis of ability and affinity to this kind of curriculum. They are not fee-paying.

So given this array of possibilities, how do you choose? I have my own opinion about private, selective, single-sex and denominational education – I'm against it. So for me, the business of choosing a school is narrowed down to which mixed comprehensive school has a catchment area that includes us. A few years ago, living as we do in North London, this gave us a practical choice (from the point of view of journey time) of about four or

five schools. Now there is only one. 'Choice', as I understand it, has decreased.

People with different principles, however, will agree with the government and consider that 'choice' has increased – but then not everyone is eligible to make the choices, for example if you don't score highly on tests or if you are not of the appropriate religion and so on. Education is fast becoming a matter of 'devil take the hindmost.'

However, there are questions that anyone looking at a secondary school might want to ask. You may not of course get true or straight answers because it is now in a school's interest to dress itself up to look better than the school down the road. Schools are now competing with each other for bright pupils so that they can score well in the league tables. But then a school with more bright pupils may not necessarily be the right one for your child, or for that matter necessarily the one that does the best job for bright pupils.

To find this out, there is one piece of information that you might like to get hold of but may well find difficult: how well does a school score with different ability level pupils? The raw data for this is only available as GCSE scores *according to pupils' 'banding' or grouping by ability when they were eleven*. If you are measuring a school's effectiveness on the basis of its GCSE results alone, then you won't know how well your child will do. Some schools get *on average* quite high GCSE results but may not do very well for one or two bands of pupil. So, for example, your child might be top band, whereas the school does very well for middle and lower bands. The average score is high – looks good in the local papers and league tables – but doesn't do too well for top ability children. Much more likely though is the other way round. A school gets very good results from its most able pupils and not so good from its middle range and low ability.

Not many areas give you this kind of information, and those that do don't help you figure out the results on this basis. You just get tables of figures. Basically, you have to make your own league tables of which schools get the best GCSE results for children in each of the three bands. You will be surprised at the results. It won't tally at all with neighbourhood gossip. And then, just to complicate things, let's say your child is high ability but is very weak in some subjects. In this case you might want to look at how well the school does with so-called low-band, low-ability pupils. Some schools with 'bad reputations' do brilliantly for pupils of low ability. It might be that the ideal school for your high ability child is the one that will do the best in bringing up his poorer subjects.

It's my view that i) all other league tables are meaningless and ii) even these more sensitive kinds of tables are limited in use because the tests that originally grouped the children according to three bands are deeply flawed, favouring certain kinds of abilities, for instance favouring a certain very narrow idea of 'reading' over other thought processes such as reasoning and creativity.

Statistics aside, what else might you want to look for in a school? Here are some questions you might want to ask of the teachers, parents and present pupils:

Does the school have a policy on bullying?
Does the school have a school council for pupils?
How often is homework set in the lower school?
How is it marked?
What happens if pupils don't do the homework?
What happens if a teacher doesn't set homework?

What is the discipline procedure at the school?
Does it work? If not why not?
What systems does the school have to involve parents?
Does the school organize foreign trips, school exchanges?
What kinds of after-school clubs and societies are there?
How approachable are the head and the deputy head?
How do open days work?
What are free-study facilities like in the school?
Is there any after-school supervision, after-school library time etc?
Does the school produce plays, concerts, school magazines, sports teams, dance displays, fashion shows, computer exhibitions, art exhibitions, local history investigations and so on?

If you know some children who already go to the school, ask to see their homework books. It is my experience that some secondary schools skimp on lower school work. They seem to be confused about what to teach in years 7, 8 and 9. Discipline is very hard to maintain in years 8 and 9. Homework is often not set, gets lost, is not followed up, is not very relevant, doesn't stretch the abilities of the pupils. Teachers are afraid to set graded homework. Homework gets set like 'Cover your exercise book', 'Finish off the work' and 'Copy out your rough work'. Very rarely will a child be asked *to find something out*. Once again teachers are afraid that this will discriminate against children who haven't got the facilities at home to do this kind of work. But then if there is after-school and lunch-hour supervision in the library this wouldn't be a problem. Or, to my mind, it doesn't seem unreasonable that children are expected to use the local library.

If I had to ask one single question about a school it would be this: How often will my child be expected as part of his or her homework to find something out? If my experience is anything to go by, it may well be hardly ever. As that is the case, I sometimes wonder what secondary schools are for. I for one want my kids to learn how to learn. If there is something they want to know or need to know, will they know how to go about finding out? Will they know how to access data? Will they know how to deal with information so that they can reason with it, argue with it, interrogate it? Will they know how to think creatively and laterally?

Even more importantly, will they want to? You can only encourage children to be like this if they have regular opportunities to *find things out for themselves*.

The question that sometimes turns out to be the most excruciating can sometimes be not what is the best school but, rather, does my child want to go to it? I notice that parents are fairly evenly divided over this one. Some parents say that their children are in no position to judge, they had better just knuckle down and take what's coming to them. Others let their children decide for themselves – a decision usually based on where their friends and/or older brothers and sisters are going. What you do really depends on how you have brought your child up in the previous ten years. If he or she is used to taking part in decisions about, say, what to do on a Sunday, what to wear, how their room is laid out and the like, then you can be sure that you'll be in for big fights if you try unreasonably to impose a school on your child. In this scenario you're in the business of negotiating: your agenda versus theirs. If you are really set on a school that your child thinks is terrible and awful then be prepared to make another visit and to have sessions with your child and perhaps other children from that school to talk about it. And vice versa: if you are set against the school that your child is rooting for, you can always let them have an opportunity to convince you.

With all the talk about academic standards it is very easy to lose sight of the fact that schools are communities and how you thrive in such places can depend on how you *feel* about the place. I'll always remember what my oldest son said to me when explaining to me why he hated school: 'It's the smell, dad.' Now, I didn't take this to mean simply the uncleaned boys' toilets, but the whole aura and atmosphere that sickened him every time he went near the place. I learned that this wasn't so much the school's fault as his own disposition at the time, but I sometimes regret that I didn't take him round some other places to find if the 'smell' there was just as repugnant. My point is that it's not only the GCSE results that need to be okay, but the 'smell' as well. To be absolutely honest I can't stand the 'smell' of secondary schools either, and have given up visiting them to do my poetry readings, but your child won't have that choice!

Clothes

I will begin with the most sensitive: shoes. I will betray my un-hip, un-clued-up approach to life when I describe a scene of some nine years ago. My oldest son and I are in a shoe shop to buy some trainers. He is twelve, I am forty. In my usual sickeningly matter-of-fact and brutal way, I tell my son what the upper limit on price is and he can choose from there. The assistant starts to proffer sample items. One of them is too small, one of them is the wrong colour but then we find a pair that fit and they are the colour that he said he was looking for.

'Put the other one on,' I say.

His face loses muscular tone. His arms hang limply by his side. He doesn't move.

'Put the other one on,' I say.

In a dull mechanical way, he puts on the other trainer.

'Walk around in them.'

He shuffles across the shop and back.

'They fit OK? Right. They're the ones. OK?'

He bursts into tears.

So I say to the assistant that we seem to have a little problem on our hands, smile grimly and retreat. Outside the shop I try to get to the bottom of it.

'What was the matter with the shoes?'

'Nothing.'

'There must have been something wrong with them. You burst into tears when I said that I was going to buy them for you. What exactly is the problem with them?'

'Nothing.'

'Is it because one of your mates has got exactly the same shoes, or something?'

'No.'

'What is it then?'

'They were Dunlops.'

'They were Dunlops? What's wrong with them being Dunlops? They make shoes don't they? Why does putting on a pair of Dunlops make you burst into tears?

Silence.

'Oh I get it. I get it. It's the wrong label. It doesn't matter whether the shoe is any good or not. It's just the wrong label to be seen in. Dunlops are wanker-label shoes, and you don't want to be seen in wanker-label shoes, is that it?'

'Yep.'

'So why didn't you say? How was I supposed to know that there are some shoes you can't wear. What happens at school if you turn up with wanker-label shoes? All the other kids stand round and jeer? And you've been one of the kids who do the jeering so if you turn up at school with wanker-label shoes they'll really go for you. Hmmm. I get the picture.'

Some parents cottoned on to this crisis in clothes about ten years earlier than me but once I realized I was no problem as a parent. I still give upper limits on prices which may well mean that this eliminates the ultra-hip, most desirable item. But that's just tough. I'm not going to be so much of a sucker for style that I have to succumb entirely. But I can face the reality of my kids not wanting to be nerds. Yes, I know I am conspiring with the style tyrants. I am bowing to their dictates. I am putty in their hands. They say: 'THIS MONTH IT WILL BE BLACK NIKES!!!' And I just roll over and say, 'OK, I am giving my son the money now, straightaway. He will do just as you say, Mr Nike. He will wear black Nikes this month. Please tell me what shoes he should wear next month and I will do my best to get them.'

'DOING YOUR BEST IS NOT GOOD ENOUGH. GET WHAT I SAY, OR DIE!!!'

'Yes, of course.'

And these trainers are truly amazing. They say they are 'engineered'. Millions of pounds are spent developing them. And they fall apart when you look at them. One game of football and all you've got on your feet is a bit of tyre tread. Another fifty quid gone. The most robust thing about these trainers are the laces. And at the time of writing, my kids are going through a phase of not doing them up. Untied laces are cool. When I was at school it was always some poor unfortunate nerd who walked about with his laces not tied up and one of the playground helpers was always tying them up for him. Now it's cool. A few weeks ago I said to one of my kids that I had just heard that they're designing some great new trainers with built-in windscreen wipers on them . . . AND HE BELIEVED ME!

It was a great relief when those big heavy leather boots started becoming fashionable. Suddenly Dad was cool too. My old hiking boots were safe, man. Smart. Wikkid. Bad. My old hiking boots, for goodness sake.

Another crucial clothes zone is the football shirt. Every year the top clubs change their strip. (Thanks a lot guys.) As summer approaches speculation hots up down our way. What will Arsenal's new 'away' shirt look like? Will they revive the old 'home' shirt? The key thing is to turn up at school on the first Monday after the Saturday that the new kit goes on sale at Arsenal World of Sport, wearing *the new shirt*. So New Kit

Saturday arrives. From seven o'clock onwards, my thirteen year old is twitching.

'Don't you think we ought to be getting down there, Dad? There'll be queues of people down there trying to get the new kit, Dad. Come on, Dad.'

'Yes, yes,' I say. 'We'll be there on time. Don't worry about it.'

A few hours later, down we go to Arsenal World of Sport. There isn't a queue. The new away strip is bluey-green. He says he wants the new home shirt. He thinks the little white collar is smart, bad, wikkid, cool.

'No, I don't want it in a bag,' he says, 'I'll put it on rightaway.' He puts the shirt on right in the middle of Arsenal World of Sport and his face goes all smiley. He glances down at his chest. He looks over his shoulder at the bottom of it. 'Arsenal' is written across the tail of the shirt. He strokes it. As we walk down the street, he glances into shop windows to see his reflection. He turns the collar up. He turns the collar down. He tucks it in, he pulls it out.

He wears it all that day. He goes to bed in it. He wears it all day Sunday. By Sunday evening it's getting a bit smelly. There are gravy stains down the front. The collar is grey. At bedtime he says, 'I'm wearing this to school tomorrow, Dad.'

'What! You can't wear that to school. It's covered in muck, it's filthy dirty. And it's beginning to smell.'

His face begins to crumple. Can he be hearing this? Can it be possible that Dad is going to stop him from wearing the new home kit on the first Monday after New Kit Saturday? His lower lip starts to go wobbly.

'But, I've got wear it Dad. It's the new kit. I–er–I . . .'

I weaken. This really matters to him.

'Look, I tell you what,' I say to him, 'I'll bung it in the washing machine and it'll probably dry out overnight in the bathroom.'

'Great, Dad. Great.'

But what with watching that old Italian film I always promised myself I'd see, and then the late-night fifties horror movie about the monster that comes from 20 million miles away (Horrible. Horrible – but fascinating!) *I forget to put the Arsenal shirt in the washing machine.* By the time I am about to stagger off to bed at two in the morning, I remember. Well, if I bung it in the machine now, at least it will show willing. It won't be dry but he'll know I remembered in the end and he can wear it on the first *Tuesday* after New Kit Saturday.

In the morning, he's up at seven o'clock. Into the bedroom.

'Dad, the shirt's not in the bathroom. Where is it?'

'Look, er, right. OK, don't get too disappointed, but, you see, I forgot.'

'You forgot? You couldn't have. You know I wanted to wear it.' The lower lip is getting wobbly again.

'Well I didn't completely forget. I remembered at two in the morning, so it's still in the washing machine.'

'That's OK. I'll wear it wet.'

By now we're downstairs at the washing machine. I take out the shirt. He grabs it off me.

'I can wear it like that.'

I'm tugging on the other end of it.

'You can't go to school in a soaking wet shirt. You'll get pneumonia. It'll suck all the heat out of you.' (It's at moments like these you start to talk like your mother.)

'Well can't we put it in the drier, then? There's time.'

'You can't put shirts like these in the drier. They're made of plastic. It'll just melt. You'd end up going to school with a little red and white ball.'

The lip is on the move again. I'm feeling the shirt now and in fact, it's not as wet as I thought. Maybe it'll dry out if I shake it a bit. So I start waving it about in the air.

'Yeah, that's right, Dad,' he says. 'Shake it about a bit. I'm getting my breakfast.'

So I stand in the middle of the kitchen waving the shirt around above my head for a few minutes while he puts his head in a bowl of cornflakes.

'I tell you what, Dad,' he says, 'why don't you take it outside in the garden? The sun's just coming up.'

'Good idea.'

So I go outside into the garden and start waving the wet Arsenal shirt around in the air. I should say here that I sleep in a tee-shirt and underpants and I haven't changed into anything else yet. So I am standing in the garden, not long after seven in the morning, waving a wet Arsenal shirt round and round in the air. Now, my neighbours know that I am an Arsenal fan. They know that I get myself down to Highbury quite often. But this? This is taking it a bit far. I imagine Tony from next door strolling across to his bedroom window, opening the curtains and looking out at his neighbour, semi-naked, in the garden at seven in the morning, waving an Arsenal shirt around.

'How's it going?' says my lad.

'Fine.'

'Great, I'll have it off you then.'

He puts the shirt on. His face goes smiley. He glances down at his chest. He flicks the collar up. He flicks it down. He glances at the word 'Arsenal' across the tail.

'See yer, Dad.'

For years now I have horrified other parents with my method of buying clothes for children. Ever since they were about five, my two older boys have known what they've *not* wanted to wear and won't wear. So when they were still quite young, the simplest thing to do was to dive into big stores like BHS or Marks and get them to choose their own tracksuit bottoms, pants, tee-shirts, jumpers and the rest. The way I saw it was that, at the end of the day, I'm not fussed whether they wear blue jumpers or red jumpers or whether some fashion nerd is going to tell me or them that blue doesn't go with orange. As they've got older, the system still applies but they're a bit more choosy about which shops. Olympia Sports has replaced C & A.

Oh, you couldn't do that with girls, people say to me. They'd just buy complete rubbish. Would they? At the end of the day, it's only clothes isn't it? I've always thought that it's more important that children get a chance to choose their own than that they wear what I think they should. I admit I nearly crossed the line and started laying down the law over the Dunlop trainers all those years ago. But never again. I mean, provided you're in a reasonably-priced shop and the kid has got the size of the clothes right, then it's no big deal what actual items they buy. Obviously, you can remind them in summer it's hot and in winter it's cold. You can say you'll need a coat, or you'll need a swimming costume, but apart from that, they seem to have always known better than me what they should wear.

My one excursion into clothes buying for them without any

consultation is when I'm in North America and come back with tee-shirts and baseball caps. I will admit here to the pleasure that I guess most parents have in seeing children in clothes they have bought for them. It's as if they are recognizing the link there is between you. I say to them, 'So you like the LA Raiders shirt I got you then?' I shouldn't be so needy. It's no big deal. It's just a tee-shirt that I happened to buy for them. It's not me they're wearing, after all. It's like the Jewish joke about the mother who buys her son two shirts. In the morning he comes down wearing one of the shirts. And the mother says, 'So the other shirt you don't like?'

An interesting crunch time comes when you think what they're wearing is 'not appropriate.' This might be anything from a near albino child refusing to wear a hat in the sun to another one refusing to peel herself out of a pair of leggings for some formal 'do' you have to go to. I remember my red-headed step-daughter saying that she wouldn't wear a floppy hat for a hike in the country on a blazing hot summer's day. So I said, 'Well, you can't come then.' And she didn't. What else could I have done? Walk ten miles and come home with a lobster with sunstroke? Weather often turns out to be the battleground. For some strange reason most children seem to think that you don't have to wear more or different clothes when it is cold or wet. They will quite happily step outside into pouring rain, sleet or driving wind in a tee-shirt and jeans. This leads to all parents' well-rehearsed pneumonia speech. The fact of the matter is that children over the age of nine are probably more robust than us, keep moving more than us and don't get quite so crotchety as us when they are cold. In addition to the pneumonia speech is the 'who has to stay at home and care for you when you're ill?' speech. It can win an extra jumper if you're lucky.

Dressing 'up' for the posh do is another affair. As it happens, in my house I'm the one who is the least likely to dress up and my children stand around pointing at me, appalled that I can go somewhere special in a pair of shoes that are falling apart or – more celebrated in family lore – trousers that have come apart at the crotch. This gives them a great sense of superiority and they can feel justly proud about how smart they look. It is one slightly contorted way to be sure that your children come out with you looking smart.

Clubs

Sorry, I can't stop to write this section because one of them's got to get to ice-skating, another one's going swimming, one of them has got to get to hockey practice and after-school drama while one of them is doing self-defence and I've got to get to my French classes and my wife has got to get to her swimming class too.

Life is a club. Every house I go in seems to be like a railway station. One child has just got in from tap-dancing, another is just off to do football training. Everyone seems to want to join something. Or does this urge mostly come from parents? 'Oh God, my child will be inadequate unless she learns the violin, goes to drama class, computer class, pottery class, singing class and swimming class.' I have a fantasy where one of my kids loses attention in the middle of swimming class and next moment he's treading water in the deep end singing: 'Lord of the Dance'. In short, things can get pretty hectic in the game of let's-develop-our-potential.

The tricky thing as a parent is to catch the moment that hits every kid: when the enthusiasm starts to wane. That moment when, instead of the busy bustle to get out the house on time, you hear things like: 'I've lost my music', 'I hope Sandy'll be there', 'I don't like the new teacher . . .' The thing is, very few kids will confront you directly with: 'I don't want to go to football training anymore', because they are afraid that you will be sad or angry that they are giving up. So they try to drop little hints, or even convince themselves that the reason for going off what was once exciting, is some little irritation like a new girl or a heater that doesn't work.

I was fairly clubbable as a child and went to a club at the Natural History Museum; I also tried the Young Farmers League, a drama club at a local theatre and even helped start up a Saturday morning football club. I died on them one by one and always sensed a disappointment in my parents that I was wasting an opportunity, not using my potential, turning into a wastrel. One phase that caused a bit of a stir came when I gave up several of the clubs all at the same time so that I could spend more time hanging about in the open sewer that ran beside our road. It seemed at the time much more exciting going for expeditions along this 'river', through tunnels, behind people's houses, than heading for the Natural History Museum or going to drama classes. But I remember it started up a whole family council of war in which my state of mind was discussed and was I going to the dogs by spending all my time with Stephen, Brian, Jimmy and Roger wading in the River Pinn. The general verdict was yes, I was.

Somehow, we have to strike a balance: introducing kids to out-of-school activities that they actually enjoy, not putting them under too much pressure and not making them feel worthless if they get bored or fed up or they find the going too tough. There are always children who do better than our own. The sickening little kid who can vault a box like an Olympic medallist, the next George Best, Jacqueline du Pré, Glenda Jackson. And that kid isn't ours. Our kids just get along OK. She doesn't speak out very well in drama class, he doesn't tackle in football, she can't do tremolo on the violin and he gets beaten in swimming.

This is OK. If they get upset because they're not the best, then we shouldn't put them through agony just to establish that they are second-rate. Yes, it can be a 'learning experience' to discover that you're no good, but not every week please. If by chance you have a child who enjoys being a tag-along, if he or she belongs to a club where who's best and who's worst is not apparent and the parents' competitiveness is somehow kept at bay, then fine, stick with it. But when the going gets tough, I say, go for the drop-out with no shame. Sure, if you want to be good at something you have to work at it. I tell them that. Though as I tell them that, I have to admit there's quite a good chance that they'll read it as me saying: 'I won't love you unless you try harder and achieve more.' And that kind of pressure destroys your guts.

Maybe your child would prefer to go fishing with you, or collect coloured stones or old comics. Going to classes and clubs is not the only way to express themselves. It is merely the most public way.

Computers

Lie 1: Computers stop children talking
I don't think I've heard children talk more than when they're talking about computers. And when you put two or three of them down in front of them, they usually gas away like crazy.

Lie 2: All computer games are about killing people
No, they're not. One of the world's best-sellers is 'Sim City 2000' and it is a non-competitive, environmental game where you have to plan and build a city. Another non-violent big seller is 'Theme Park'.

Lie 3: They can't use computers for creative things
This may be because you haven't got the right programme, or that you haven't shown them how they could use it. With one of the simple children's graphic programmes or, better, with an adult system like 'Claris Works' children can draw and design anything that will fit on to an A4 or an A5 page. They can make greetings cards, labels for their rooms and toys, funny letters to people, party invites and, when they get homework, all their home projects. With 'integrated' software like 'Claris Works', that is to say a system where you can mix a page of writing with drawings, diagrams, graphs, spreadsheets and databases, then virtually any kind of printed page is possible. There are also simple animated cartoon programmes. The problem is that very few children get shown how to do any of these things. If you are in any way serious about your children's literacy in the 21st century then this is the stuff to get engaged in, but boy, it costs!

**Lie 4: Real computers for word-processing, designing and pro-
gramming are really for adults and children ought to keep their
hands off**

Children can get going on real computing as soon as they can hit
the keys they intend to hit and follow through the consequences
of their actions. This is probably about three years of age. There
are some excellent programmes, like Kids Pix that helps children
to make, design and draw things. As for older children, I met a
German boy of fourteen who had spent three or four years devis-
ing various language games by programming them on an IBM. In
schools, they should be buying in scanners and a form of the elec-
tronic pad with a stylus that enables children to make coloured
newspapers and magazines with photos, coloured drawings and
the like. Computers are not only adult toys.

Dad

Suddenly, Dads are political. Politicians, not usually celebrated for their willingness to put in hours of parenting, are grabbing headlines telling us that civilization will fall apart unless fathers step in. It is always much easier to come up with snappy generalizations about what other people should do with their children than include in the frame our own hesitant, muddled ways of getting by.

But as we are on generalities, I can't resist sticking my oar in. In France, from 1914–50, there was a severe lack of fathers – millions were either in the army, dying or dead. If a severe lack of fathers was the sole cause of poverty and crime then France in this period would have been in anarchic terror. It wasn't. We bring up children in many different ways and in many different contexts. A single-parent family with no help from relatives is different from one with help and money. One man who calls himself a father might beat his children, never cuddle them, never talk with them and rarely see them because he is out, while another father might be very jolly and loving, but only in the holidays between terms at boarding school. The term 'father' is becoming less and less useful a way of describing what is actually going on in the relationship.

My position is this: a really bad father is worse than no father. There isn't anything morally superior about a family simply because it can claim to have a father attached to it. Put another way: for centuries, many families only stuck together because women were financially helpless. It seems that what is happening now is that women are becoming more financially independent and are looking for better reasons to live with men than waiting for them to bring in the money. Fathering could, in the past, be used by men as a way of exerting power over women and children. This is not to deny that many women and children liked it like that – it was a kind of unwritten contract. The crisis now is that these unwritten contracts are being torn up as more and more women discover that they don't have to be in the old position of dependence. The problem for many men is that we don't know what to do. One obvious thing is to grab a microphone and say that single parents are causing the break-up of society. This makes us feel needed. Another response is to say that men are in pain. (*In* pain, not *a* pain.) This is the argument that says men are damaged by society telling us that we ought to be providers and defenders. And when all these media images show powerful men smashing their way through life, we try to live up to it and suffer as we fail.

The problem with this is that it ignores the 'net effect'. That is to say, there is a kind of final sum, a total picture that we can make of the effects of turning out men and women the way they are. No matter what difficulties 'new men' are saying that they face in the world, we can't escape from the crude maths of violence. Under the headings: Rape, Murder and Assault, we know that men outscore women by millions – whether that be for violence to women, other men or children. Whatever it is that is causing this, we can't escape from the fact that it must have something (not everything) to do with how men become men. The mere absence of a father will not do as an explanation because we know that plenty of violent men were brought up by violent fathers. As I said before, a horrible father is, conceivably, worse than no father.

So what follows is not meant to be a way of prescribing what a model family should be or what the ideal father should be, or for that matter, why the ideal man should be a father. Some of us choose to be fathers and wonder if we could do it any better; some of us become biological fathers and wonder whether there is anything more we could do if we wanted to; some of us are excluded fathers and are desperate to get more of a look-in; some of us are fathers who exclude ourselves and thank every day that passes that we don't have to do any more than we do; some of us have all these feelings all at the same time. Part of the problem is that there isn't much of a society-wide debate about fathering. Women have magazines, and daytime radio and TV frequently makes the assumption that it is talking to women. The magazines that men buy tend not to mix in little tips on fathering. When exciting innovative programmes have men-only discussions, they spend much more time talking about erections than talking about a common long-term result of putting an erection in a woman's fanny – children. Fathering in our culture is represented as a dull, slightly absurd activity, closely linked to dandruff, porky waistlines and steamed-up glasses. Think of dads in British sitcoms. For centuries, mothering has been portrayed as the fulfillment of womanhood, brave, selfless, loving. There is, of course, an argument that mother-worship is pernicious, glamorized rubbish meant to tie women to saucepans and nappies. For all that, it can be taken by women who want to do so as something positive. Where are the positive images of fatherhood?

Liberal American movies and soaps frequently have father-son buddy moments where, say, teenage boy gets into trouble at school, rows with mother or step-mother, and then nearly dies in a car crash. Dad suddenly realizes that this was a 'cry for help' and rushes round to the hospital, puts his arm round the son's shoulders and says, 'I've done it all wrong, haven't I? I just haven't been there for you when you needed me kid. We're going to make this thing work, son. Let's go to the ball game.' Run credits. The point is we don't get to see the actual dull day-to-day business of fathering. That'll take place in the rosy future. There are some good father-brutes in literature, men like D.H. Lawrence's father in *Sons and Lovers*, and in films there is often time for a bit of paternal hell-raising. There's been a few films recently which raise a laugh from guys looking after babies, but the joke here is either the old gag about babies being little puking-peeing machines or what a weird thing it is to have sexy guys looking after them. *The Cosby Show*, self-consciously trying to tell black men to stay at home, love home and study, put in a weekly slug of good-image fathering. But it always struck me as immensely un-difficult. When things got sticky they just sat down and talked sincere. The point I am labouring here is that fathering doesn't sell tickets and put bums on seats. It just happens, or doesn't.

So here are a few thoughts on fathering:

1. Dignity is dead. All the years you practised looking cool, hard, sober, sexy, dashing and profound are over. Just don't try it on. Your kids will take the mick something terrible, you will become depressed and will sue for divorce on the grounds that your children laughed at you.

2. Companionship is OK. In spite of much mockery of trendiness it is quite possible for fathers as well as mothers to be friends with their own children. This doesn't mean trying to keep up with the latest slang, the latest children's TV programmes or the latest trousers. Just simply being there is much more important. Some of the best dads I know are slobs who hang about a lot. Yes, possibly driving their wives mad with their lack of ambition or with their lack of housework, but at least they are there when the whatsit hits the fan. At least they listen when the kids have something to say.

3. Don't always be in charge of the discipline bag. Everyone in this world will want to manoeuvre you (the male) in to being Mr Discipline, the one who sorts it out in the end, the final arbiter, the umpire who delivers the final judgement. If you take this on, you end up undermining your partner and boosting the idea that it's only men who can sort things out. Then instead of everyone wanting you to be Mr Discipline, you get it in the neck for screwing up and thinking you're a big I-am.

4. Don't dodge it either. We can't do the opposite and say, 'Oh I don't want to be a big bad wolf, I'd rather be a little pig.' It's as bad to be under-powerful as over-powerful. It completely disorients children if we don't mark out the limits of what is OK. It does them no good to have an adult who can be railroaded and ridden over. It scares them to think that you might be weaker than they are. Some new man dads think they can avoid all unpleasantness and all harking back to the bad old authoritarian days. But we can't avoid it because children use us to find the limits. These limits don't have to be old-style 'No talking at the table, no laughing in the front room' and the like. It's my feeling that the most important limits to mark out are not so much the finer points of etiquette and manners but much more the ones of *mutual* respect. It's 'I will listen to you, if you will listen to me. I will take care of your things, if you take care of mine. I won't interrupt you, if you don't interrupt me. I will listen to your side of the argument, if you will listen to mine. I will help you tidy up your room, if you help me clean up the kitchen.'

Discipline

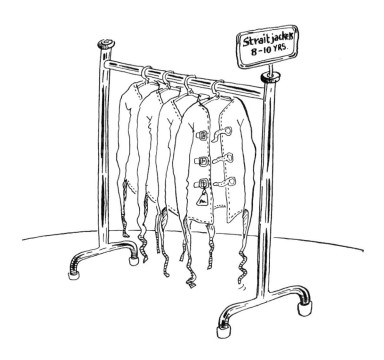

The nastiest way to discipline children (or indeed anyone you're in a loving relationship with), is to suggest that your love is conditional on them behaving in certain ways that you think are right. 'If you clear the table, I will love you. If you fail at school, I won't love you.' It's the tyrannical side of love. It's how we try to control loved ones. Our parents did it to us, so unless we make a conscious break we tend to do it to our own children. In between we do it to lovers.

I'm not going to pretend I'm immune from it, or that it's possible to completely eliminate it as a way of going on. But as a starting point it's quite useful to think about how as children we were treated that way and how since then we've carried on this behaviour. The reason why it's so pernicious is that if it's a regular and usual system of child-rearing it leaves children never knowing for certain that the people who have the prime job of looking after them, actually like them. Existence becomes a matter of panic and duty. Panic that no one likes you. And constant pressure to perform in order to win the unattainable. Such children grow up with bottomless pits of need inside them: need for reassurance, need for affection, need for reward, need for appreciation. Of course, we all want those things and much-loved people need these responses and feelings as well. The difference is that much-loved people are more likely to feel satisfied and safe when they receive affection and appreciation, while the person for whom love is conditional is never satisfied, never convinced, never reassured.

As a system of nurturing it has been around for several hundred years and is by no means dead. It was the way many of the middle-class virtues of moderation, thrift, industriousness, sexual abstemiousness and ambition were instilled into children. Life was divided into virtuous and sinful activities, and you got love for virtue and hate for sin. It is different from living in a permanent state of not being loved, or from being on the receiving end of brutality and abuse, because it is disguised as love. It sometimes appears as satisfying affirmation only to be snatched away in the form of dislike. When you put a group of children together you quite quickly find that some children are much more concerned to win your approval than others. Some children can't wait for you to reassure them that you are going to enjoy working with them and struggle in the first few seconds to win special approval. And it never stops. The bottomless pit is open wide the whole time. These children have been disciplined through conditional love. They don't know if they are worthwhile human beings. They don't know whether anyone can be trusted as a real friend.

Discipline is making sure that children don't disrupt and spoil the lives of the people they love, and the people with whom they have to co-exist in order to keep body and soul together. For discipline to work, it has to go on within the context of the child knowing that he or she is loved. The disciplining shouldn't endanger that. We have to remind the child that when we get angry with them this is not the same as hating them. When they think they have failed at something, we have to remind them that this hasn't affected our love for them. Alternatively, when they succeed at something, this doesn't mean that they have become more lovable. These things have to be said over and over again. They have to be explained or they will be in doubt. And doubt is corrosive. There are millions of people walking about who were never told by their parents that they were wanted or loved or nice. There are millions of others who were only told they were loved or nice when they dressed in a certain way or came home from school with good grades. Many of these people spend much of their time doubting their worth and, by projecting it on to others, doubting other people's worth.

So discipline is not, as popular newspapers often imply, a series of acts that will produce certain desirable effects. The same act in one home will have a different meaning in another. Yelling at a child who knows for certain that she is loved will be different from yelling at another who fears that she has never been loved. Both may be devastating and shocking. Both may have the immediate and desired effect of stopping the child drawing on walls but at a deeper level very different things are going on. The first child may be horrified that the parent could be so angry but it doesn't take long for her to see that this was only over the single deed and not a general across-the-board dismissal. The second child may be less horrified by the yelling but simply take it as further confirmation that she is worthless. All discipline takes place in a context.

But people still want to know what works. You hear people saying, 'I've tried everything but he still does it.' 'What can we do? No matter what we say, she goes on doing it.' 'He doesn't listen to me.' Once you've lost the use of withdrawing and giving love as a means of control then what have you got left? Walloping, sanctions, reason and separation. To cement these you've got contracts, deals and ultimatums.

WALLOPING is brilliant in the short term and completely useless and counter-productive in the middle and long term. It gets quick, immediate results: the child stops because you're hurting her. If it doesn't hurt the first time then you can make it hurt more, which is the same principle as torture. In the middle term it scarcely ever works because the only real message the kid has got is that if you get caught you will get a wallop, so the best thing to do is not get caught. Anyway, most wallops don't hurt so much that they don't wear off after a few minutes or few hours. In the long term it doesn't work because all you do is pass on the message that the solution to problems is force. This means that a child who is walloped goes about walloping other people. It gets quick results. So walloping produces a splendidly useless vicious circle in which nothing is solved.

I have walloped my kids on various occasions. The worst time was when I got back from Australia and I hadn't seen two of my children for about three months. So I took them on holiday. The younger one, who was eight, spent most of the first two days saying he didn't want to do this, he didn't want to do that, that everything was horrible and he didn't care anyway. Finally, I lost my rag completely, put him over the bed in the hotel room and walloped his bum. I then told him to stay just where he was and went out of the room with his older brother. It was awful. Terrible. No use at all.

Looking back on it I can see that it was born entirely out of two people's frustrations, neither of which were being talked about. So it ended in violence. He was cross that I had been away and my taking him on holiday hadn't allowed him the space in which to say that he had been cross. So he used the occasion to be anti-social and to punish me for having been away so long – a familiar scenario when parents have been away, or even when children have been away. Reunions are fraught with naughtiness and little acts of punishment of adults by children – refusing food, punching younger brothers and the like. But what was *I* doing wrong? I had wanted gratitude for my big-deal act of generosity, taking them away to a hotel. I had wanted them to be pleased to see me and pleased with this treat. But that was only my selfish scenario and when one of the boys didn't perform as I wanted him too, I lost my rag and punished him. What I should have done is first of all ask him what was bugging him and if he couldn't express it to use a bit of nous and guess that he would want to show his anger that I had been away.

The other thing I've done with my children is less violent but more sneaky. It's the use of over-vigorous handling: the extra-firm grip of the arm, the grasp of the back of the neck, the tweak of hair. It happens at that crunch moment when what you have said has had no effect whatsoever, that whatever is driving you nuts is so engrossing to the child that you use force to extricate them from it. Underused, and only in extremis, I can just about justify this. You have said to your kid that yes, we will go round to Lucy's house but the deal is that we have to leave at four o'clock to be sure of picking up Jim on time. At four o'clock you get up to go and your kid throws a tantrum, says she isn't going and starts yelling. You can say, 'Right, we won't be coming to Lucy's again.' When this doesn't produce a result, you say, 'Lucy's mum wants you to go too, it's not just me.' You say, 'Remember the deal? Leave at four to pick up Jim. It's not fair on Jim either. You are not getting anywhere having a tantrum and it is now five past four.' In these circumstances I have picked up the child, still screaming, now biting and kicking, taken him or her to the car, stuffed them in the car seat and driven off. Is this use of force justifiable? I would say yes because the deal was clear, the reasons were given and they were fair and necessary. There was no physical pain involved.

I've seen the situation of the child who doesn't want to leave – and plenty of others like it – where parents have just capitulated to the child. The parents don't want to make a fuss in a public place. They are afraid to be seen in public showing force and overriding a child's wishes. They don't want to sour the outing with a punishment. Poppycock! The unpleasantness is in the child's tantrum, breaking of the deal and the ineffectiveness of the parents.

SANCTIONS means the withdrawal of treats and life-enhancing pleasures. Imposing such sanctions has the side-effect of reminding children that life-enhancing pleasures are not there by right but are only possible because of agreements between people. Every conscious child has treats and pleasures. If deals and agreements are broken we can say, reasonably I think, that a given treat or pleasure will be taken away. Children go to clubs, have outings, pocket money, TVs and hi-fi systems in their rooms. They expect to be allowed to go to parties, have friends round, visit special places. If our children break a deal then any one of these pleasures can be withdrawn. However, I don't think they can be withdrawn as a punishment when no deals were struck in the first place and the child wasn't given a warning that this would be the punishment. That strikes me as unfair. So the deal is that, for example, if she keeps nicking her sister's scrunchies she won't be able to go to drama class. She does go on nicking the scrunchies, so she doesn't go to drama class for a couple of weeks.

PURE BALD REASON with no sanctions, I must admit, has not been very effective. Maybe some people are better at it than me. I have tried the long questioning sessions in which I try to find out *why did you do it* and *didn't you know what the consequences would be?* and *I can understanding why you did it but there were all sorts of other things you could have done instead, weren't there?* The most famous episode in our house was when my step-daughter was about twelve. I was sitting looking out of our back window when I saw a funny looking bundle in the honeysuckle hedge. I looked a bit closer and saw that it was a sandwich in a clingfilm wrapping. I know what's happened here, I thought, the kids have been mucking about in the garden flinging sandwiches about. One got caught up in the hedge, they couldn't see where it had gone and so they left it there. I know what I'll do: when they get back from school I'll give them a whole number about how food costs money and if they would like to buy their own food then they can feel free to throw it about, but for as long as they are dependent on us for their food, then they should either eat it or give it to someone else. The boys came home first and I pointed out the sandwich in the honeysuckle hedge. No, they said, they had never seen it before, but it did look quite funny stuck there in the hedge didn't I think? Then the step-daughter came home. Did she know how the sandwich got there? She looked at it closely, then blushed.

'So, this is your sandwich, is it?'

'Yep.'

'Crazy question coming up here, love: *why* is your sandwich in the hedge?'

'I put it there.'

'Another crazy one coming up: might I ask *why* you put it there?'

'I didn't like it.'

'OK, let me get the picture. You got up yesterday morning and came downstairs to make your packed lunch for school. As you know, you don't have to have packed lunch, you can have school dinners, of if you prefer you can take a quid or so and buy some chips and if you really, really don't want to eat at midday you could just buy a drink. No one makes you take sandwiches. And no one tells you what to put in your sandwiches. If there's anything that you want us to buy for you to put in your sandwiches, you give us a shout. You know all that, don't you?'

'Yes.'

'So you make your sandwiches, you go to school. At lunchtime you sit down to have your sandwiches and you then decide you don't want them, so you put them back in your bag. You don't give them to one of your friends. You don't even throw them away, so as to hide from us that you didn't eat them. On the way home you pass many rubbish bins but you still don't throw away the sandwiches. You come home. You walk past the dustbin at the gate without putting the sandwiches in there. You walk past the bin and the black bags in the kitchen and you don't put them in there either. You go to your room. You open the window and throw the sandwich out of the window. It lands in the honeysuckle hedge. You leave it there. Have I described what happened?'

'Yes.'

'Last crazy question here: do you have any idea why you did all this?'

'Nope.'

No matter how I went through the story, I never got even the faintest inclination as to why she did this. So how do you deal rationally with it? How do you reason with her when you can't get to the bottom of motivation or intent? I don't know. In its own way it's hysterically funny. Other people might see it as a cry for help, perhaps: look at me, I don't know what I'm doing. So if you think that throwing sandwiches out of the window is generally not a good idea, how do you get her to stop doing it? Punish her for the crime? Or invent it as a new crime with a new punishment and get her to agree not to do it? And should a few hours be spent on i) explaining why making sandwiches only to throw them out of windows is a waste of food and money; ii) trying to get to the bottom of what's bothering her? In the end I think we did all these and were proud of progress until we found dozens of rotting sandwiches stashed away in the bottom of her wardrobe. New deals were struck, new sanctions invented. Ho hum. Nothing is simple. Life should not necessarily be seen as progress. It can be seen as a spiral, a zig-zag, running backwards or a bog.

Finally, SEPARATION. Americans call it Time Out, from the penalty systems in American sports. The principle is the same. The child is giving grief. You or other children may be getting riled. What do you do? Wallop, reason or sanction may not be the best thing because what the child is actually enjoying at that moment *is* riling you or the other children. More attention and aggro through walloping, reasoning and deliveries of sanctions may be delightful to the child. It makes the temperature rise, it holds your attention, it holds everyone's attention. The punishment becomes the pleasure. Some kids feed off such punishments.

Here the resource you have is Time Out. You withdraw the child, physically if necessary, from the scene of the aggro whether it be other children or yourself. You put the child into a dull place. This can work very well if it isn't overused. It doesn't always work. Resourceful children use it as an opportunity to get on with a bit of drawing, singing, beating out a rhythm on the wall or making scratching noises on the floor. But even if this is the case it has the short-term effect of relieving you of the cause of the aggro and it also means: that you mean business when you say no; that certain kinds of anti-social goings on aren't acceptable; that the child understands the meaning of the sentence: 'you know what happens when you behave like that don't you?'

The real test of your resolve on Time Out is when you are out at a friend's or in a café or museum, because real Time Out in these situations is back home and into the sinbin. Can you do it? I wish more parents would. I can't think of the number of times I've heard parents in public places saying: 'Don't do that again, dear. If you do I will get angry. No, don't do that. If you do that again, there'll be trouble when you get home. Look at the bird dear. Don't do that. Do you want a sweet? Look at this piece of paper, it's interesting isn't it? Don't do that.' When I see people doing this I want to say to them, 'Look, all you have to do is be bold once or twice and say, "OK that's it sunshine. I warned you. Out. In the car, back home and you go to your room. We talked about this before we came out. We talked about what you did when you were at Uncle David's. You're doing it again. Home."'

This may well cause massive wailings and gnashings, fists flying at the parental bum but once practised a few times, it works wonders. It goes into the repertoire of things to remind the child of when the going gets tough: 'You remember what I had to do that day at the zoo?' Yes it may wreck an outing. It may even wreck your whole day. But what is one little day compared with years of making your and other people's lives a misery? We have to make it clear that there are some things we don't want to put up with and, believe it or not, we don't have to put up with.

Divorce and Separation

From a child's point of view break-ups are very powerful evidence of their own powerlessness. By splitting up, parents prove that children have very little say in how the big, basic things in their lives are decided. Two adults who were looking after them in one home suddenly, sometimes without giving any very understandable reason, stop living in one home. New bedrooms, new brothers and sisters, new adult carers appear – and you didn't have any say in any of it. It is also evidence that parents will do what you always suspected or feared they might, which is die, disappear or reject you. The reason why they do this is possibly because you are not nice enough. Break-ups can very easily get interpreted by children as proof that they are unlovable and helpless.

Unless we do something about it.

Whatever happens separation will be a shock and it will disrupt lives. Right from the beginning we have to make it clear to children that i) we are not breaking up because of them and ii) breaking up doesn't change what we think of them. Saying this over and over again needs to be accompanied by actions that prove we mean it. No matter what conditions we are living in after the split, it is much more important that we share these with our children than try and shield them from it. You might be living in some sort of temporary accommodation, a flat share, or even back with your parents – it doesn't matter. If you try to keep your children away from it, or to protect them from it, they will interpret this as rejection. They might even moan and complain and say that the conditions you are living in are terrible and they don't like it. It doesn't matter. Just explain that that's the way it is at the moment and you are working to make sure that it won't always be like this. The reason why they're moaning is probably much more to do with being fed up that the family has broken up, rather than with the actual material conditions of life when they are with you.

After a break-up we may well have to devote hours to reassuring behaviour: hanging out together, playing deadly board games, watching telly together. Don't try to palm them off on parents and friends. Prove that you want to stay being their parent. This doesn't mean showering them with bigger and better presents or taking them out to bigger and better places. Far better to keep the treats at the same level as they were before and up the amount of human contact between you.

The whole question of divorce and separation is bedevilled with notions of failure. We have a way of talking about relationships as 'successful' or 'failed'. This always strikes me as particularly unhelpful. It means that there is a relationship league table in people's minds and we grade each other according to how 'good' we are at conducting them. The problem with using the language of success and failure when talking about relationships is that it leads people to see themselves at times of break-ups as having failed. It follows from this that people look for someone to blame. Whether this turns out to be yourself, your partner or both of you, I would suggest is not helpful to you, your ex or your children. The whole spirit of failure and blame weighs people down, prevents them from carrying on, leaves people without hope. Instead, we should learn to accept that in life we have relationships that begin, have middles and end. For some people they only end with death, for others they end because we no longer need each other enough to go on living the way we were before. I would say that no matter how badly you think your partner has behaved towards you, it is not useful to you or your children to get into a spirit of blame about it. The situation was created by both of you coming together, it takes two to tango.

Take this as an example: Dave and Susan start to have a relationship. Dave has a daughter from a previous relationship whom he sees regularly. He lives on his own. Susan has a son from a previous relationship who lives with her all the time. A lot of the first few months of the relationship is taken up with discussion about 'your place or mine'. They like each other a lot but neither wish to take the plunge and actually move the underwear and CDs into the other person's place. Both like their independence and the space of their own flats.

This goes on for a couple of years. There are a few niggles about why one has to do more of the shunting than the other. Why one has to do more step-parenting than the other. Now comes the crunch. Should they live together? Long discussions take place about where, how, when, schools, disruption, financial arrangements and safeguards. Progress is zero. One of them makes a move: it happens to be Dave. He says that he's going to buy somewhere new. It'll be big enough for all of them, but it would be even bigger if Susan chipped in her share. It doesn't work out. Dave gets the place, Susan doesn't join him. End of story.

Not so fast. Susan discovers that she is pregnant. Susan feels that Dave ought to come round and discuss this. The relationship didn't formally end, so it could resurrect itself around the baby, couldn't it? Dave says, sure, come and join me in my flat. No, she won't. Things turn nasty, they have rows. But Dave keeps coming to see Susan, takes part in birth preparation classes, is present at the birth. Now what happens? Dave says that he wants access and wants to put in some child care. He wants to be a father. She says, piss off, I don't want to see you again and I don't want you to have any part in bringing up the child.

There now follow years and years of dispute, going to conciliation and the courts in order to solve the matter. Each sees the other as behaving unfairly. They blame each other for what happened. Each thinks that the other is using the child as a way of getting revenge for having made the relationship 'fail'. They sometimes badmouth the other in front of the child. They try to enlist the support of the half-siblings as well as the child itself in what has become a real tug-of-hate. The children are confused, blame themselves for what is happening and swing violently to and fro in loving and hating each or both of the parents.

I don't pretend to have any solution to this. Two people who started out having some shared hopes and aims grew to find out

that these hopes and aims didn't coincide enough to make living together possible. Then, I would argue, because we live in this culture of seeing relationships as a matter of success or failure, it turns to blame and recrimination. Somehow those two people are going to need to find some way or another to accept what happened, to see that they were both involved in something that couldn't work because they were both the people they are (or were). Then they can ease up on blaming each other and ease up on using the child as the means by which they can get revenge.

Millions of us are bringing up children in non-nuclear ways. In spite of what the conservatives (small c) say, life has always been like it. For hundreds of years, women had to bring up children without soldier, sailor and contract worker partners being there. Millions of men and women died young in wars and industrial work. Children have always been brought up by people other than their biological mothers and fathers. Uncles, aunts, grannies, nannies, boarding schools, reform schools, navy schools, 'the old lady down the road', foster parents, orphanages, workhouses, children's homes have brought up millions and millions of us. Meanwhile, many so-called nuclear families disguised the fact that one or both partners were having sexual relationships with lovers, servants, mistresses and prostitutes and an enormous amount of child care was being undertaken by people other than the biological parents.

We don't have to be ashamed of what is happening now. It seems to me that people are trying out ways of living and bringing up children that are, if anything, more honest than the old 'have-it-off-with-the-maid-under-the-stairs' method or (so as not to be sexist about it) 'having-an-affair-with-the-milkman' method. But we can't help children to be secure, hopeful and capable people if on the one hand we don't want a nuclear set-up (or can't have it even if we do want it) while at the same time filling the air with ideas of failure, blame and revenge. Children are damaged by that.

Exams

As this book's cut-off point is adolescence, the exams we're talking about here are school tests, SATs and the exams and tests that are given to children while learning to play music, do gymnastics and the like. All children will get some form or another of test-itis. The form of one of my children's test-itis is to pretend that the test isn't happening. He keeps saying, 'It's OK Dad, don't worry. Sure I know it all.' When the results come out and they are not as good as they should have been, he says, 'I did as well as I could have.' Other children display more conventional forms of test-itis, not sleeping, dithering, dropping things, crying, shouting at people for no reason at all, blaming other people for having lost things and so on.

We are mostly dishonest about testing children. The main

reason for testing them is so that we adults can feel good. We like the idea of being able to grade them, put them in classifiable chunks. It ties them to our way of classifying each other, and wrenches them out of their more anarchic ways of relating to each other, based as they are on affinity and affection. So we rank them according to age and/or ability and put them through tests. This delivers them up to the adult world marked for life as being either capable or (more usually) incapable. People see themselves as fitted to do one thing rather than another on the basis of what is sometimes a very narrow idea of proficiency or failure.

So when we enter children for tests, why don't we say all this to our children? We can be honest and tell them that mostly the test is there not to help them. When they get the results they may not even be told where they were good and where they weren't. Even if they are told this, they may not be helped in trying to improve their weak spots. And they may not have needed the test in the first place to arrive at this understanding; they could have simply talked about it with a teacher or parent. Instead of which they got anxious and experienced failure.

People say that tests in music and swimming give children incentives and rewards. Of course they do. But that doesn't mean that is the only way for children to develop interests. How many people are there in the country who were put through their music grades up to the point of complete loathing and now never touch a musical instrument? Music grades, like all tests, are devised by adults who are good at what is being tested. They want to spot the next generation of people who will be as good as they are. The tests are not there to encourage as many people as possible to take part in and enjoy the subject or pastime. I think we should tell children this. Sure, take the tests if you want to, and your music, swimming or gymnastics teacher wants you to, but this is not the only way you can take part in this activity. Or, alternatively, there are plenty of other activities that are test-free: knitting, painting, drawing, writing poetry, dancing, reading and so on.

School tests are a different matter. There is much less choice about them. My own feeling is that most of them are completely pointless and produce many more people who think they are no good than people who see themselves as can-doers. If tests discourage rather than encourage children to learn, and to take control of their own learning, then they are worse than a waste of time: they are positively harmful. Take spelling tests. Each week our children come home with lists of words. They struggle to learn the spelling. Is there any evidence that this has any long-term effect on whether they can spell well or, more importantly, write with confidence? No. What usually happens is that the children who read a lot and see their parents reading and writing a lot are good spellers and the ones who don't are bad spellers. There are always exceptions: there are highly literate middle-class parents worried that their children – often boys – can't spell. Learning lists of words is no use because it doesn't deal with the problem. It might indeed be contributing to the problem. The lists are often of words that are similar but with key differences. Words that end with -ent and words that end with -ant, for instance. Plenty of people will remember that the list contains certain words but find it much harder to remember which word was an -ent word and which one was an -ant. They blur and merge. When faced with things that we don't like, it is much easier to forget than to remember. The brain tries to avoid the unpleasant route. We can threaten and cajole children and tell them that they won't get on and get a good job and be nice, successful people like their parents if they don't knuckle down

and learn the words. They might even learn them well enough for the test, *but there is no guarantee that they will remember them in a year's time.*

This is because many tests divorce information from the context in which it is easily understood. So, for example, words are best understood in sentences, stories and poems. If parents and teachers 'teach to the tests', they quite often make the subject harder because it is less meaningful. The children become worried, more aware of themselves as potential (and actual) failures. If you have brought your children up to argue and debate, to value personal relationships, to understand the world as full of ideas and processes that link up with each other and aren't just chunks of facts, then it may well be that they are very bright and no good at tests. I remember having spelling tests at school where we weren't told either what the words meant, or even how to pronounce them. So when the test came you might hear the teacher read out a word and you'd sit there thinking, 'That one wasn't on the list was it?' This has happened to my kids and the lists that they bring home from school. OK, so we are literate parents and we sort it out, but where does this leave the parents who don't speak English or aren't particularly literate?

We can help children with tests but it is a soul-destroying experience. My children have sometimes banged their heads on the table, roared, torn up pieces of paper and accused us of being spineless collaborators with the system – or words to that effect. They were right. That said, we can show children how to learn things by:

- reading the particular passage (or list!) over and over again
- getting them to talk about what has to be learnt, discussing what's difficult and why
- inventing little dodges and ruses on how to remember things, such as mnemonics (a rhyme or other device to help memory), and finding patterns and connections
- showing children the method of learn, cover-up, test, check. You sit and learn. You cover up the passage you have learnt. You recite it. You check where you've gone wrong. Learn, cover-up, test, check. We tell them that they have to do this four or five times before they'll get hold of it and then we can test

them to see if it's worked. When we test them, then we can test them in a different order from what's on the page. Have a laugh. Get the child to test you to see if you can remember it. Try to 'socialize' learning by sharing and talking about the material that is being tested. It makes the whole thing less lonely and less of a strain.

As parents we should try not to get racked-up and tense about tests. It's not us that's taking it. When and if they fail, don't go into blame mode. We shouldn't make our affection for our children seem dependent on success or failure. It will eat away at a child's sense of worth. They will come never to appreciate what they do themselves; it will never seem good enough because we always wanted a bit more. Our job as parents should be to help children cope with success *and* failure. We can remind them before and after that failing or succeeding will make no difference to how much we care about them. We can reassure them that we still love them, even when they become depressed. Or big-headed. When they decide to jack in music grades and gymnastics medals we shouldn't make it seem like they're going to lose a bit of our love. We shouldn't make music practice and swimming training seem like things that they are doing to keep our love. We can ask them their opinions about this: 'Are you doing this for me? Are you worried that I'll be sad and won't like you so much if you don't go in for Grade 2 violin?'

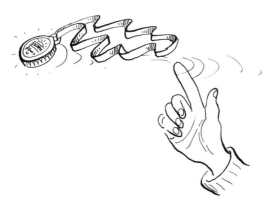

Food

Shakespeare got it wrong. Music isn't the food of love, food is the food of love. The snag is that we keep thinking that food is food. As adults we buy food from shops, cafés and restaurants and these acts have very little to do with love. As parents we provide food for children to eat, as children we are given food and this exchange has everything in the world to do with love. This means that whatever goes on in the interchange over food is some kind of reflection of what the relationship is about.

Think about all the things we do with food and children – and the things they do to us. We urge them to eat more, less, more quickly, more slowly, more of this, less of that, more often, less often. They on the other hand, refuse this, ask for more of that, leave bits of that, refuse to share some of this, hoard some of that, ask for this to be made differently, in the old way, in the new way. Usually we think all this has something to do with what the food is intrinsically like – its flavour, its consistency, its heat or what-ever. We negotiate with kids about taste and cooking and timing.

Much of this may well be missing the point. What really may be going on in the child's mind is: do you love me? Or: I am going to test whether you love me. Or: I am going to punish you for not loving me as much as him. I am going to punish you for not coming home earlier. Do you love me enough? I love you but I don't love your new partner. I miss my mum. Each of these thoughts can translate into I don't want any of this, or, I want some more of that. Why don't you cook some of that other stuff again . . . and again. I know it takes ages but please . . .

When I moved in with my second wife, one of my boys was about five years old. He had a little routine when food landed on the table. He would look at it. He would ask whether it had this or that in it. Then he would say, 'Did you cook it, Dad?' If I had he'd eat it; if it was cooked by his new step-mother he wouldn't. He was so upset and cross about the break-up and my new relationship that he would regularly refuse food that my wife had cooked – even though he had eaten it when he knew her as a friend a year or so earlier. Only Dad's cooking could be trusted.

One of my children tends to get constipated. No doubt there are all kinds of metabolic and constitutional reasons why one person tends that way and another doesn't. If you don't do a lot of physical exercise, it's harder to get your bowels moving; and clearly some foods tend to make us more bunged up than others. But there's also the psychological element. How do you view a child who knows that in order to make sure she doesn't get constipated she must eat certain kinds of things every day, but even in complete agony will still refuse to eat high-fibre food? Of course you can think of it as a purely physical problem and jam the kid full of laxatives, and because she goes regularly, something has been solved. But clearly, something else is going on: all kinds of issues may exist about not wanting to take full responsibility for her own body, using the whole matter as a way of saying take more notice of me, and no doubt others I haven't thought of.

The more we make ourselves slaves to children's every taste and whim the less satisfied they will be. If children don't help with meals, don't lay the table, clear up, chop vegetables, fetch and carry shopping, they can use the serving up of food as a means of using power. And they do. I sit down at a friend's house and a meal is served up. One of the kids says: 'Ugh! Don't want that.' This is done partly to impress me, and partly to hurt Mum or Dad by saying I can make you look less powerful than you want people to think you are. If she had helped with the meal then the display would be less likely to happen. Her comments might also be generally ruled out of order because no one should be free to treat someone who cooks someone else a meal in such an ungenerous, unappreciative way. As you can point out, you may or may not like the food, but remember it gets here because someone has worked to put it there. If you don't like it, we can talk about *you* putting in some work, to make something that you prefer.

Should you force children to eat food that is good for them? If food becomes a battleground, there is every chance you will lose and the child will try his or her hand at eating disorders. So how do you make sure a child gets a balanced diet? Encouragement and participation.

- **Encouragement** is putting less than expected on the plate, suggesting ways of mixing foods on the plate, telling stories about foods you hated when you were a kid, making mealtimes good times.
- **Participation** is telling kids what's in foods, why we eat this rather than that, what one kind of food does for you and another doesn't, getting children to help with meal-making, serving and clearing up – boys as well as girls.

Yes, yes, we do all that, but what do we do when he still says he doesn't want fisherman's pie? First of all he's got to be polite about it or he'll get nothing to eat. Then he can eat something else provided it's got a bit of protein in it and plenty of complex carbohydrate (in other words the nutritional equivalent of fisherman's pie) and provided *he* makes it. A peanut-butter sandwich, for instance. If we run round after one kid making special exceptions you end up on the road to ruin. They will use every mealtime as an excuse to prove that you are their slave. There are times when the conciliatory method – make something yourself – is used by one child to get one over the others: 'Look at me, I get special treatment.' If it looks like that then you have a midway position and a tough position. Midway says: 'I'm going to put some on your plate, you can eat some and leave some but you're not filling up on biscuits later.' Tough says: 'Tough. That's what I've cooked, that's what you're getting. You don't have to eat it but there isn't anything else.' This needs nerves of iron because you have to be consistent or the whole scheme will fall apart. You have to follow the thing through and not dish out Mars Bars later. It leans towards the battleground approach unless you're quite jolly about it.

When you visit other people's houses, you can demand of your children that they don't make any rude comments about other people's food, they say please, thanks and no thanks and give things a try even when they have big doubts. No sane friend is going to go nuts if a kid of yours gives things a try but doesn't like it. We've had a boy from abroad staying with us on an exchange. It seems that when he's at home his mother is his slave, he gets preferential treatment over the other children, has his own pot of honey that no one else is allowed to touch and from which he can eat any time he likes. If food lands on the table that he doesn't like, he starts shouting and abusing his mother who rushes out to the kitchen and finds something else. If she makes something slightly out of the ordinary he pokes it and pulls it, asks what's in it and then usually refuses to eat it. When he came to our house he started to do the same sort of things.

Interesting times. First of all he discovered that he had to start laying and clearing the table. Then he had to get his own breakfast and clear it up. Then the routine with the main meal of the day was that he didn't have to eat it if he didn't like it, all he had to do was get himself some bread and cheese or fruit or salad and eat that. Immediately there was a crisis. Faced with pasta and pesto he got very twitchy and started poking the pesto pot. We suggested that he try a little. He put some on his plate and said, 'How shall I eat it?' We suggested he use his finger. He did, thought it was awful and had plain pasta and cheese. Then, as the children tucked into their pasta and pesto, the smell began to get to him so he said he would give it another try. He liked it and ate it. Away from all the love-me, hate-you games of home and his special privileged position he started to discover that he doesn't have to be such a weak, dependent sort of person.

Finally, I mentioned that we should tell children what's in food and what it does to our bodies. We can't do this unless we know! At the risk of being obvious: every day we should have some fresh food, some green vegetables, some protein (fish, meat, beans, cheese), and plenty of complex carbohydrate (potato, pasta, rice). We should avoid too much fat and sugar of the sort you find in chips, biscuits, butter, margarine, fried food, sweets, hard cheese, cake, chocolate, crips and most canned drinks. There's probably not much point in simply telling children that they've got to eat this sort of diet without explaining why. That is: that the body needs certain foods or it starts conking out. For more details, loves, let's look at a book . . . That sort of thing!

Friends

The eight years or so of life covered by this book are crucial for one thing above all others: making and losing friends. It is the key time when children learn (or don't learn) how to establish relationships away from home, away from parents. We all of us remember: it can be bliss, it can be hell, it can be bliss *and* hell. In fact, it's not much different from the friendships and enmities of adult life.

I can remember how pleased I was on finding a real friend when I first arrived at secondary school. He seemed to enjoy the same jokes, know the same Yiddish slang, his parents came from the same part of London as mine. Then suddenly it all crashed. I did something to offend him: I sat with someone else at the school concert. He instantly stopped talking to me, cut me dead. I was left high and dry: I had put all my eggs in one basket and had only really made friends with him. Another boy who had come from the same primary school as him took me to one side. He had seen what had gone on. He had seen the way my friend had dropped me just like he himself had been dropped for me a few weeks earlier. 'Don't worry about it,' he said. 'Paul's like that. He's all keen and matey one moment and the next he sulks and drops you. He's always been like that.'

I hadn't met anyone like Paul before: so emotional and temperamental. I didn't know how to handle it, other than to start knocking about with some other kids. I was upset and I don't think I believed what his old friend told me. It was also class news; girls in particular were interested. Weren't him and me a team that had seemed to be making waves as in-guys? It was good gossip. I didn't share the problem with my parents or my brother who went to the same school. I put a brave face on it and just got in with a big crowd playing football and 'Off-ground He' in the playground. The crowd (about six or seven boys mostly from the same primary school) were kind enough to take me in, though it was obvious I was a refugee, and obvious that they had-n't been my first choice as friends. For a few days I would watch Paul out of the corner of my eye to see how he was making out. Who was he playing with?

In the end, he relented. He deigned to talk to me again. But of course he had blown it. He knew that I wasn't a wreck. He had tried to use freezing me out as a way of wielding power and con-trol. I didn't know it at the time, but I did the right thing – only possible because his old friend gave me some good advice, and the big crowd had let me in. If either of these two had been nega-tive experiences I would probably have been in a bad way. As it happens Paul and I went on to be great friends. He always went in for sulks but either or I or someone else could usually shake him out of them. He learnt it off his mother who used sulking as a weapon against her husband and children when she couldn't get her own way at home and everyone used to walk about under a cloud while she got over it.

I'm not sure how typical this story is but my impression from my own children is that for them it's sometimes been better, sometimes worse. The hardest things they've had to cope with haven't been, as with me, one individual child who is a very close friend and then uses his or her position to get control. Rather it's been the problems of there being an in-crowd and how to get In when there's someone who doesn't want you In. Or you're In, there's someone who's Out and she tries to get at you by lying about you to some of the others who are In. In other words, the power games are played out in groups rather than pairs.

Children can find this, at times, quite frightening. It can feel as if suddenly one moment you've got a whole crowd of friends and the next you've got no one. Or sometimes it gets really hot and sweaty on the inner ring of the in-crowd with who's coming round to tea, who isn't, and who mustn't be asked, so that life gets quite tense. It's the kind of thing that is captured well in stories like *Blubber* by Judy Blume or the *Malory Towers* books by Enid Blyton.

I don't think it's any less emotional for boys. One of my chil-dren spent a few weeks, if not months, trying to get in with the in-

crowd who were playing football, but a newish tough lad in the class had managed to get a little gang round him and told my son that he couldn't join in. Our boy didn't tell us about this for a whole term. He presumably couldn't bear to voice out loud the humiliation that he felt every day when he tried, and failed, to join in the game. There were some painful little sideshows as well. A friend of his who had come to the school only recently had got in on the game but he hadn't helped our lad in too, and hadn't stood up for him either. Presumably the way to stay in with the gang leader was not to cross him by suggesting an out-kid could become an in-kid. Needless to say, our son felt betrayed by this. But there was also the sad fact that our boy didn't go off and find someone else to play football with. Why not? Because the other kids were out-kids too and no one wants to play with them! So all he ended up doing was yearning to be more in, to win back his old friend, and avoiding other kids because like him, they were low status and might further jeopardize his chances of getting in. They might contaminate him with their out-ness and he would be confirmed as the lonely nerd. Meanwhile, in the in-crowd there were individuals who our boy thought were his friends, who had come over for tea, who had invited our boy to birthday parties but when it came to football couldn't or wouldn't include him. It's a sorry tale that, even as I write, is not wholly resolved.

How should a parent intervene here? Very easy to weigh in and wreck everything. Make him look like a weed because he needs his Dad to sort it out. Yet at the same time you don't want to leave him coping all on his own because quite clearly he is going under. The key thing is to find some leverage that will break the hold that the in-crowd leader has over all the other boys. My plan, as I write this, is to talk about it to his class teacher. I gather that there is one day of the week when the whole class has entitlement to use a particular space in the playground and yet the leader still manages to exclude my son on that day too. Surely, this is where an intervention can safely be made: our lad is as entitled as any-one else in the class to join the game and the in-crowd leader will have to just knuckle under and take it.

But oh dear, it's so intense. It matters so much. I can remember another time when things were getting so keyed-up with one of my other children that moves had to be made to tone the whole thing down. No, you don't have to go round to tea with her tonight. No, you don't have to sit next to her all the time. Try play-ing with someone else for a bit. A larger in-crowd emerged. It seemed to work for a while but there was clearly pain from one or two girls on the outside who started telling lies about girls on the inside as a way of trying to get recognition.

It's hard to know what to do. It's very easy to fan the flames or put big parental feet in when kids will gain more self-knowledge and more skill in forming relationships if you don't. For us there is the problem in knowing that the ways in which our children make and break relationships is itself related to how we have treated them within the family. We know that the bullying, hec-toring kid may well be someone who is cowering and weak at home, or that the kid who first appears most friendly becomes the most needy because no one notices her much at home . . . and so on. So this makes us a little bit anxious. Ways in which we are getting it wrong will manifest themselves in the problems our children encounter with others. Oh no! All will be revealed! True, but getting anxious about it won't help, nor will too much inter-vening to 'improve' our children's relationships in order to allevi-ate our own self-doubt.

Gender

Anyone who brings up children knows that no matter how important we are, or how important we *think* we are in the way we affect and influence them, we are not by any means the sole influence. It's very easy, and I'm as guilty of this as anyone, to put such an emphasis on what home, parents and family do to children that it can seem as if the home environment is the cause of everything. That way, we take the credit when our kids do well and we take the rap when things go wrong. When youth crime, teenage pregnancies, (or anything seen as a social ill) increases it must be parents' fault.

This really won't do as a way of looking at the world. We don't live in little boxes sealed off from each other, nor is society made up of a big wall of these imaginary little boxes. We all live, work, think and love in several kinds of places: workplace, home, school, in front of a television, while being treated for illness . . . Then again, we are often described as consumers, but we can only be consumers if we are also producers and earn enough money to consume something. Or again, we see ourselves at various times as belonging to a class, a club, a religion, a nation, an ethnic group, a gender.

I happen to think that the starting point for all this is to look at how society is organized to produce all the major and basic things we need: electricity, buildings, food, transport. Without these we have nothing. But to get them, some people have a lot of power, some less and some virtually none, at least as individuals. Power in the wider world is shared out very unevenly. Children know this. They might not know it or describe it in the way I am doing here, but they know it simply by going to school, the doctor's, the shops, watching TV and of course, watching us. In other words, no matter what we might *say* there are always these real situations that children live in that affect them. You or I might think it highly desirable for a child to learn that whacking someone over the head in order to get his or her own way is not the ideal way to go through life but thousands of books and movies suggest the opposite, and there might even be someone in school or in the neighbourhood who is doing just fine by whacking people. Conversely, a parent might encourage a girl to believe that she need not get a job because if she plays the game right she can hook a guy with enough money to keep her. Meanwhile, she sees female teachers, doctors, TV presenters every day, and may well know female role-models who have worked outside the home for most of their lives. What one can say with certainty is that there is never a perfect match between what we might say at home about ideal boys or ideal girls on the one hand and what our children see and do in reality on the other. And of course there is probably just as big a mismatch between what we as parents say and what we do.

This is all by way of saying that there are no certainties for parents here: neither the one of so-called 'traditional values', nor the one of feminism and gender equality. Many of us can think of children from highly traditional homes, in which the gender roles were very fixed, and yet the girls have grown up to be career women and the boys have turned against traditional male authority roles. But for the past few years, there's been the new phenomenon of parents who have tried the ideal of gender equality, and are finding that their girls spend whole weekends painting their nails and their boys want to kill rival football fans. These differences can't be explained away simply as revolts against the home, though of course that does happen and, interestingly enough, seems to be happening to children at an ever and ever lower age. (More 'outside' influence, perhaps.)

What seems to be happening is that although we are miles away from equal opportunity in all walks of life whether it be industry, the professions or politics, women overall have increased the amount of time they spend in paid work. The public face of women has been one of greater frankness and confidence in saying what they want. This impinges on children very directly from their mostly female teachers, TV, film and magazines. The young women's magazine that my sixteen-year-old step-daughter brought home recently had a problem page that explained how to masturbate your boyfriend and how to get him to be careful when he stroked or masturbated you. Girls today live in a world in which, no matter what we might say or do as parents, it is considered quite normal to say what you want, expect a lot and to talk about it quite openly and publicly. The agony aunt's replies to the girls' questions about boys and their penises were humorous, irreverent and undeferential. Basically, the message was that you don't have to do what men say you should.

All this might seem a long way from, say, five year olds playing with Lego or singing in the school choir. Not so. Children are less insulated than ever before. They absorb all forms of media, they wear adult-looking clothes, they have older brothers and sisters, they go out with parents to football matches, pubs and hotels. The new ways in which teenagers and adults gender themselves are having profound effects on young children too.

I took my ten-year-old step-daughter and her friends to see the film *Mask*. The story concerns a nerdish bank clerk who finds an old mask which has the power of enabling him to realize his desires: he can become a superb dancer, a Rambo, a Mr Cool and so on. The female lead is tall, blonde, muscular and busty. Several people get to wear the mask in the film, notably a crook and a dog, both of whom are male. When we came out, my step-daughter said, 'Why couldn't the woman have worn the mask?' And one of her friends said, 'I wonder what she would have done . . .' There was a thoughtful silence.

It occurred to me that this was a question that very few girls or boys thirty years ago would ever have thought of asking. I definitely didn't think of it after I saw the film. And it's interesting as a question about desire and power. To rephrase my step-daughter, she is opening up questions about the nature of female desire, why wasn't she allowed to see a film that could show this, are there films that show this and so on.

But if girls are moving on and grabbing more space, demanding more of everything, how are boys and men responding? At the moment, none too well. There is no sign of violence to girls and women showing a big decline. The political, managerial and professional classes seem very slow (and resistant?) to correcting the imbalance; the amount of childcare and housework that men do doesn't seem to have increased very much. Boys in playgrounds still try to kick girls off the football pitch even though it's the girls' turn; they can quite calmly explain to you why girls are less intelligent and less able to perform tasks such as car maintenance even though they have seen examples.

There is a new school of thought that wants to see this male supremacism as another form of victimization. It's pointed out that many more men die from male violence than women and that statistic rests on millions of incidents in which men feel that they have to challenge each other with fists, weapons and guns. The educational statisticians are now claiming that boys are doing worse than girls in school. In the past, where films, books, TV and newspapers have lovingly described girls' and women's sadness, the new critics claim that this has overlooked boys' and men's pain at, say, having to prove themselves and failing, whether it be in sport, war, work or sex. In fact, the argument goes, even the winners are in pain because they are under so much pressure – why else the drugs in sport, the film-stars' crack-ups and the like?

As a parent, we are just as likely to have to spend an evening listening to tears and sadness from a girl about, say, the way she has been frozen out of a group of girls, thinking that she is not pretty, as from a boy who has been bullied, thinks that he is a wimp, can't score goals and the like. Clearly, quite a lot of this sadness is anxiety about fitting an ideal. Saying that the pain of boys and men is equal to the pain of girls and women misses the point that we are going through a time of massive change. Girls and women are staking out new claims. Boys in playgrounds are threatened that girls are being given one day in five on the football pitch. They get angry in classrooms that girls are claiming an equal say and they are getting frustrated that girls in general want to work harder and muck about less. It may well be that this experience is an entirely foreign one to most parents.

In the arguments we get into with our children that involve gender, we should probably bear in mind that there are two movements going on here: girls rushing forward and boys digging their heels in. It seems to me that the biggest difficulty is that whereas girls at present have a whole raft of desirable aspirations on offer – women doing their own thing, getting what they want, earning money, looking great – boys have, by and large, only got the old ones of macho and management – play more football and/or become a judge or an expert. People made a great fuss about Paul Gascoigne crying in the World Cup and some people cited this as an example of new-manishness. The only problem with this is that it overlooked the fact that Gazza was crying about football, not over the fact that, say, his father had died or that his girlfriend had dumped him. We haven't found ways (and not many people are looking) for boys to see non-macho roles as desirable. It's possible that new woman, on the back of her new-found freedom and power, will force it upon us and thence on to our children. Meanwhile, it seems to me that as parents we do owe it to boys, and indeed everyone, to help them find something attractive (or at least necessary) about non-macho activities.

End of theory. Now for the practice. We are still living in times

when we have to remind girls over and over again of the things they *can* do. It is amazing how often you hear girls apologizing their way out of taking up opportunities, and not grabbing what's on offer. Without putting them under undue pressure to succeed, we can support girls in saying, go for it, of course you can do it if you want to, don't give up. It's clear that one of the ways that sexisim works now is through a channelling of women and men into different professions and activities, primary school teaching being one of the most obvious to children. We can say to girls that they don't have to think that they can only go in for 'women's things'. We are living in a no-holds-barred time and if there is something that she wants to do, or even wondered if she could do, we can say, yes, sure she can. Girls' and women's team games are no longer confined to hockey and netball. There's no muscial instrument that a woman can't play, whether it be an electric guitar, saxophone or drums. There's no subject at school that is more for boys than girls. Computers aren't sexist.

Meanwhile for boys, we can say that they can and should hold the baby, change a nappy, do the washing up, hoover the passage, write thank-you letters, send condolences to relatives and friends and so on. Boys need to be reminded in particular of how homes are places where jobs have to be done and it isn't the God-given job of sisters and mothers to service them. Boys can cook, wash and shop as well as anyone. I think there's space here for fathers to change in the way they treat boys. Many men find it very diffi-cult to show affection to their boys by hugging them, being nice to them, telling them that they love them. The old-style gruffness and pat on the back are still very much in use. They can be junked. It is OK for lads to sit on dads and for dads to kiss lads goodnight. We can say that they look great in their new trainers. The word 'sissy' can be banned, it's aimed at terrifying boys away from being pleasant, affectionate, warm and quiet. Skill at sport does not have to be a matter of being horrible to other people, it can involve pride at being good, pleasure in increasing skills. We can emphasise this with our boys, even though other parents may be running up and down the touchline screaming, 'Kill him, kill him.' For people who know their football, the contrast here is between Pele and Cantona.

Going Out

We live in curious times: children know more about adult life than ever before, largely through TV and their own chat. They are once again, after a gap of some two hundred years, dressing like adults, hanging about adults 'til later at night, having more money to spend, and yet . . . many children are less free than they were forty years ago. I can remember going on a bus with my friends to the pictures, the swimming pool, to see other friends, from the time I was about nine. I don't think I know anyone, myself included, who would let their children do that today. So there's a contradiction here: children are more knowing than ever before and yet more protected.

I don't think this matters all that much. Life is full of contradictions. I don't see any problems with children knowing about sex and war and most of the other old no-nos provided they can be talked about within a safe and secure environment. And though it can be really inconvenient, there isn't anything wrong in making sure that your children are safe in the outside world. In fact, part of being safe is learning about what you are being kept safe from. So this leaves us with two obligations: to talk about the world like it is, without euphemisms, and to be around as chauffeurs and chaperones for trips and outings.

The going-out routines in families are subtle barometers of change. When our children are very young we all just assume that to 'go out' is to go out with a parent or adult friend. England is a particularly horrible place to do this because there aren't enough places and entertainments that are child- and family-friendly. You can live in parts of the country where there are hardly any film shows, theatre shows, restaurants, fairgrounds, theme parks or zoos. And where there are, the prices are frightening. Because we have devised a culture that sees 'growing up' as growing better (even though all the evidence points to this not being the case) we have turned children into lesser beings. It doesn't make any difference that rationally we all know that we were once children, that we can all remember how important our lives were to us then. Collectively as adults we have constructed a world where children don't matter very much. People who entertain children are often regarded as jokes, failures, rejects from adult entertainment or, like Blue Peter presenters, simply waiting to get a break into adult presenting later. Teachers are particularly reviled. Nursery school and infant school teachers are thought to be less important than secondary and university teachers. I could go on, but those of us who are parents and want to find interesting and child-friendly things to take our children to, have to face up to this again and again. How often does the local arts

centre put on shows suitable for all ages? How often do town leisure and arts committees arrange family entertainments? How well geared up to family outings are English Heritage and National Trust sites? The answers to most of these questions is: not very much. The daft thing is that we feel pathetically grateful when a little is done.

Meanwhile, out we go with our children hoping for the best. Half of us are walking about thinking that other people's children are badly behaved hoodlums and the other half of us are thinking that our own children are badly behaved hoodlums. So what with blaming your own kids, blaming other people's kids, worrying that someone is blaming your kids or that fun-loving singles, aged bachelors and retired school teachers will thump them for laughing in public spaces, going out with children in happy-go-lucky England can be a very tense experience.

We were lucky enough to go to Australia with all five of ours and, though it was hard to put a finger on it, we soon discovered that they've got a different attitude to children out there. Maybe they're just lucky enough to have the space and sunlight to allow children to run about more. Maybe it's because Australians are generally less stuffy than we are, so children spilling things and shouting is less of a problem. And maybe Australians can afford to be more relaxed about their children because they provide better facilities for them in public places: climbing frames and 'flying foxes' in parks, massive sports facilities and sports festivals for girls as well as boys.

So what are we entitled to expect from our children when we go out? And how do we get it? Beforehand it's Little Talk Time. We have to make clear what is definitely not OK. This has to be agreed by everyone and if it's broken then the trip comes to an end. This may sound fairly drastic but the alternative is that children regularly use the public arena to test the limits of your power to control them. They think that in public you will be less prepared or less able to be in charge. Or to put it another way, behind every child's act of naughtiness is the concern that you are not strong enough to look after him or her. A vicious cycle of anxiety and naughtiness sets in. A child being horrible to his mum and dad, getting away with it, running around being horrible to other adults and children in the vicinity, is a child who is deep-down worried about whether anyone is strong enough to look after him.

When I say strong, this isn't anything to do with physical strength, and it has nothing to do with being so controlling that a child has no freedom and no autonomy. After all, you're aiming at a situation where a child in public is behaving OK because he or she wants to and feels safe enough to do so.

So you set down the rules which must, as a minimum, be that you don't break other people's things, you don't burst in rudely on adults' conversations whenever and however you want, you play fairly with other kids, that if there are rows and fights with other kids you find an adult to sort it out, you don't say other people's food is rubbish or muck, you don't make massive amounts of noise just because you're outside your own home. OK, these are the rules, agreed? If when you turn up at the castle, museum, café, granny's place, football match the rules are broken then you have to, repeat have to, jack it all in and come home, even if it means some sacrifice on your part. It's hard but I've found it's the only way you can stop your children wrecking your life in public places.

That said, you have to play fair. You can't just go to see any old mate and sit there for hours gassing away and expect your kid to abide by these rules. You have to ration out adult chat with child-centred activity, while pointing out (boring, Dad) that you are trying to be fair.

And so to going out on their own. Perhaps some of you reading this don't let any pre-teen child go out on their own. I understand that. We've all heard too many reports of children and teenagers being snatched only yards from their own homes, on the way home from school, or going to the local shops. Even with this terrible threat, I reckon it should be possible for two, or better, three friends to go out together on their own. Of course there have to be conditions and advice galore. They must stick together, they must discuss with you and with each other what they would do if approached or attacked. They must stick closely to the planned itinerary, and make phone calls to say if there's any reason why they are late. And no negotiations over the phone about staying out later, stopping over and the like. All that has to be sorted out before.

I've discovered this last is one of the most important because what these twelve year olds figure out is that mums and dads are much more likely to say no to extensions and extras when you are in front of them before leaving the house. Once out and on the road, they think that you are a softer touch and you will agree to anything. If you are, stand by to be rudely awoken to hearing that the kids did something that you hadn't agreed to and wouldn't have done had you known about it. Examples I know of: the girls went to a late-night disco, the boys went to an evening football match, they went out and bought a bottle of this and a bottle of that. These pre-teenagers spy a weak spot, aim for it and go straight through into the forbidden. The deal has to be step-by-step towards full independence with everyone knowing what is going on. My experience of twelve year olds is that quite a few of them want it all now and if they can't have it, try out little plots and schemes to get it. The most fruitful moment for this, they think, is on the other end of a phone line, outside the cinema or round at Sam's place. 'Sorry sunshine, the deal was eight o'clock back here. That deal still stands. Any deviation means no sleep-over at Sophie's next week. See you here, as agreed, at eight o'clock. Bye.'

When they come back you may get the I-live-with-Hitler treatment: 'You don't ever let me do what I want to. All the others are going. They think you treat me like a baby. But I'm not. When I have my own flat I'm not going to invite you round. You can keep your big noses right out of my business then, I can tell you. What did you think I'd do? Take drugs, have sex, get drunk?'

'Just before you got back I checked with Hannah's mother and Jamie's father and Maria's mother and they all said they were coming straight back home. As far as I can figure out, it's only Georgia who will be going.'

'So? Who do you think you are? Spying on everything I do?'

'Oh, only a parent under contract to land you in adulthood in one piece with some of the apparatus necessary to run your own life. Apart from that, no one important.'

'Yeh, yeh, yeh, no one's laughing. Not funny.'

Good Times

Books like this are always in great danger of seeing life as though it was one great problem. Everything can easily seem as if it's a matter of making impossible choices, facing awful dilemmas or being just plain awful. Living with children as they grow comes to seem like an obstacle course. But it isn't. Or if it sometimes seems like that, it needn't always.

If I had to say what the point of having children is, then somewhere near the top of the list I would say, it's so that you can have good times together. Some people might say things like, having children is about leaving something behind, making a mark on the surface of the earth that you can say you made, having someone to care for you in your old age, keeping the family name going, keeping an idea or a feeling alive into the next generation and so on. I can't say I care much about any of these. For me, as I say, having children is about having a particular kind of good time.

Good times with kids come in many different shapes and sizes: pulling through an illness, going to the cinema, playing beach cricket, seeing them asleep in bed, collecting them from school, listening to them being cheeky to you, playing Snap, telling stories, singing, visiting a museum, watching them in a nativity play and so on. I'm not sure that we can expect children to be grateful to us for these good times, or necessarily to recognize themselves as fortunate for having them. While they are still very young, we can perhaps expect them to thank us for putting ourselves out, to appreciate that most pleasure requires a bit of effort by someone to make it happen. But any true sense of how important and rare real good times are might have to wait until much later, or even not until we are dead and gone. This is not because children are little egocentric sods but because it is very hard for them to compare and contrast their way of living with other people's. They just don't have the necessary life experience. And it's a bit of a pain to wind up a blow-out at an ice-cream parlour by saying: 'The children in Ethiopia don't get treats like this, you know.'

Some people feel resentful of their children that they are having more treats, more good times than they had. But, to state the obvious, that's not the children's fault. We can't lumber them with our old stuff. If we have good times with our own children, there's a good chance that they will find ways of having good times with their friends, lovers, spouses and children. At the end of the day, that's the only reward we are entitled to in this game. All the gratitude in the world can't possibly be worth the knowledge that our children are capable of finding more ways to be contented with life than us. This isn't meant to sound either glib or easy. Often, the sadnesses or difficulties our children will face

as adults are because of unforeseen circumstances: loss of a job, a bereavement, an unlucky break or whatever. The idea of all of us moving towards universal happiness just because we have good times with our kids, is of course absurd. I would seek for a better deal for everyone in how we organize society, but that said, I think it's a damn good idea to remember that we only have one life and that the more unselfish pleasure we can squeeze into it the better. It seems to me that that is something we can usefully and enjoyably pass on to our children by having plenty of good times with them.

Grandparents

I have heard many nightmare stories about grandparents: the grandmother who comes in and says that you don't know how to bring up your children, that your children are ugly, rude, stupid, untidy, dirty and will end up on the scrapheap of life. This is said in front of the children so as to make them feel terrible and you useless. There's the grandfather that tries to wish on to your children team sports, boy scouts, brownies, boys' brigade, army cadet corps, the territorial army, Sunday school and other nation-saving activities.

It's clearly very hard for parents to tell their parents to get knotted, especially if you're trying to get as much baby-sitting out of them as you possibly can. You can't have it both ways. If grandparents do loads of grandparenting then they also have the right to do loads of grand-interfering. My children and step-children, who have a potential quota of ten grandparents, have ended up with one fairly regular one and the rest distant or deceased. Other people I know have four rock solid regulars. No pattern emerges, no handy stereotypes of loving grannies and doting grandads with pockets full of sweets, cracking corny jokes. The strange thing is that we all go about merrily using the word 'family' (as I do in this book), when in actual fact, your family and my family may be utterly different units, with different patterns of child-care and ways of earning money and doing housework. Grandparents in some families are key players, with children living up to half their lives 'round at nan's', while for others, seeing grandparents is a boring if not painful ordeal that happens no more than once every two months. Clearly there are no ground rules, we are in a state of great change and variation.

Words like 'family', 'granny', 'nan', 'grandad' – quite apart from Dad and Mum – are now used to describe such different kinds of roles that you can never be sure in conversation that you are talking about the same thing.

In the face of this, there's much more making up of the rules as we go along. What is absolute routine and gospel in one family, hasn't even been heard of in another. Sunday dinner every Sunday round at nan's, says one family. We visit grandma once a year in the summer holidays, but not if we can help it, says another.

And because we are ourselves children, we have our duties to our parents. Some feel entitled to as much attention as we give our own children. Some grandparents think it is wrong for their daughters to take full-time jobs because it means that they won't be caring enough for them. And being old is no joke in a declining welfare state. Old people I've met who have no additional means of income, feel cheated and angry. They load some of this on to their children and even their children's children. Many feel unloved and unappreciated. Though it's not entirely rational, I've heard old people say over and over again, 'You wouldn't be here if it wasn't for me. I scrimped and saved to put you through college. Your father was in the war you know . . .' and so on. It may be partly true but it doesn't mean it's very easy to listen to. With the arrival of company pensions and private pensions, the old contract between the working generation and the retired generation has been broken. The working generation is no longer paying for the retired – it is paying for itself. Even if the present working generation haven't figured this out, the retired generation has. Our parents know that we are not paying for them anymore. Phrases like an 'ageing population' and 'tax burden' keep cropping up. We are talking about people here, our parents, the ones who may be irritating us to hell on a personal basis partly *because* of their wider worries.

As far as I know the United Nations has not drawn up a grandparents' charter. (The UN children's charter, by the way, is well worth a read.) What would a grandparents' charter have to include? Grandparents are entitled not to have their houses marauded and wrecked by grandchildren. Grandchildren are entitled to some no-strings affection from grandparents.

Grandparents are probably not entitled to totally no-strings respect for all their ideas but then that doesn't mean they should ever have to put up with gratuitous rudeness. Grandparents who offer no-strings affection are likewise entitled to give grand-children ludicrously inappropriate, out of fashion, embarrassing presents *and be thanked for them.*

Deep down, having children is a way of being a child again. Every time you do a parental thing, you are drawing on the rela-tionship you had as a child with your parents. No matter how hard you might say you're doing something different or starting afresh, it's inevitably influenced by, a reflection of, or a reaction against what happened to you. Every time I speak to my children I can hear my mother and more usually my father inside me. Sometimes the words shape themselves. Then my own children spot their grandfather's phrases and intonation, jokes, slang, swearwords and quotations. They say, 'That's a very Harold way of speaking Dad.' In close-knit, cross-generational families such as, say, Indian families, this would be so obvious it wouldn't be remarked upon, but with the looser, western set-up this is a dis-covery that our children can make. They start to see links between generations not just in family likeness, but also in interesting cul-tural ways. I like that.

Holidays

Choosing

Have you noticed how we spend September? Listening very carefully to other parents to see if they have managed to crack it: how to have a trouble-free, enjoyable family holiday in which everyone's needs are satisfied and no one's labour is exploited? A simple list of requirements, isn't it? No rows, no one (usually mother) feeling that she is doing even more work than she does at home, and everyone having their disparate interests catered for: fishing, football, boy-watching, girl-watching, bird-watching, sandcastle-making, mountain climbing, arcade-game playing, sun-bathing, TV viewing and so on. Can it be done? Is there a family that has managed to pull it off? If so, we all want to know. What's the secret?

Instead, in September we swap horror stories about our teenagers trying to jump out of the car on the autobahn, mothers breaking-up fathers' fishing rods, fathers climbing mountains with a group of children and getting lost in storms, babies getting sunstroke. And those are just the enjoyable bits. Like so much else in this game, it's a juggling act, with the extra spice that people who don't usually spend 24 hours a day in each other's company for more than a weekend at a time are now having to do it, in confined spaces like cars and chalets, for anything up to month. Oh boy!

My rating as a family holiday-maker is bad. I am excessively selfish, requiring unreasonable amounts of anti-social time stuck in front of the box watching the Test Match; I experience sudden bursts of energy when I revive old longings to climb mountains and then resent the fact that young children can't walk more than twenty-five yards; I have sulking sessions when I regret that we

84

aren't in a remote French village; embarrass everyone with exhibitionist musical outbursts in cafés; and insist on long expeditions to hunt for second-hand books. This kind of behaviour is fairly intolerable and leaves the children wandering about hoping that I'll climb out of my egocentric bubble for long enough to play the occasional game of cricket with them in a muddy field.

Having quite a gang of kids, we've had to think of holidays that allow older children space, time and possibilities for making off into the distance, while younger ones can mix hanging about and playing with excursions to farms and beaches. This leaves the little matter of us, the adults, who start to feel nasty and resentful if only children's interests are catered for and we can't visit that incredibly interesting neolithic lump of earth or that medieval cess pit. In fact, my children have a cruel take-off of me, hand on chin, eyes narrowed, saying in a squeaky professorial voice: 'Do you realize, kids, that that stone was put there over a thousand years ago? Mind-boggling . . .'

When it comes to choosing holidays, I will admit to being a bit of a dead loss. One place, however, that seemed to supply almost everything that everybody wanted was the Isle of Arran. The older kids could hire bikes and go pony-trekking – they could have gone sailing, windsurfing, diving and mountaineering if they'd wanted to as well. The younger kids could play on beaches, visit ice-cream shops, go on nature trails, play miniature golf and get to know animals on open farms. The adults could climb mountains, see old historic sites, ride on paddle steamers, go deer-spotting. As a special treat for refugees of the sixties, there were several folk concerts where, as one of my kids sang it: 'Three crusty geezers all with a beard. Three crusty geezers all with a beard. Three crusty geezers they're worse than we feared.'

I'm not going to say it was totally pain-free. At dusk, clouds of midges descend on you and try to eat your lips. They can be kept at bay, just, with pungent lotions. But there were extra bonuses: an agricultural show, the Highland Games and pub quiz nights – though now I come to think of it, we always lost these because we didn't know the answers to questions about old Scottish recipes.

The place that seems to have scored most highly with everyone, apart from me, is Centreparks, a chalet camp with cafés,

restaurants, swimming pools, pony riding, and all kinds of high-ly desirable activities available under cover in great glass geo-desic-type domes. I don't go a bundle on this form of communal pseudo-rural holidaying: they remind me of woodland shopping malls. But my family tell me that I am a spoilsport, don't appre-ciate jacuzzis and squirrels and what's the matter with you, you like pizza don't you? I will concede this: Centreparks are brilliant in quick bursts. You probably won't be able to afford any more than that anyway.

Journeys

When it comes down to it, the worst thing about holidays is getting there. Martians are reported to be in hysterics every summer watching urban humans planning quiet, stress-free holidays, but beforehand squeezing themselves into small metal boxes for many hours of noisy, stressful travel. Some holidays are little more than periods of recovery from journeys. How many times can you say to two children biting each other on the back seat: 'Look out of the window, there's a tree!' The Walkman was invented for car journeys though, and many hours of peace can be won with the right tapes. But now I come to think of it: one is never enough is it? Because they argue about what to listen to. Maybe they will design cars in the future with back-seat audio sockets, like on aircraft, for in-flight entertainment. I could patent that as a 'desirable accessory'.

One solution I tried for the food and drink problem was for them to make separate picnic lunches (*and* teas, dinners, snacks and afters). The idea was that they wouldn't have to nag us or complain because they were each responsible for their own pack. Apart from a bit of raisin-throwing and drink-carton squeezing, it was quite a good system. In fact, I'm not sure why we stopped doing it. Maybe having five children in the kitchen just as we were packing up to leave was a disincentive. For smaller families it's a goer. I should patent that as well . . . Kidz Journey Boxes. Needs a snappier brand name, but the idea is spot on.

By the way, have you noticed that the wind in lay-bys always blows towards the road? This means that when you get out of the car and stand with your four-year-old son trying to direct the pee at the embankment, it flies straight back at you. So he unloads his bladder all over *your* trousers. Thanks son.

Whoever is driving needs a strong left arm and whoever is in the front passenger seat needs a strong right arm. This is so that when the going gets tough and the noise level has reached Heathrow Terminal 4 proportions you can stretch behind you, without looking, and get in some good clumping. Wave the arm around a bit and yell a few horrible curses and the noise usually dies down for a few minutes.

If things get bad on small, quiet roads – 'Nearly there. This is the last stretch, don't spoil it now, darlings' – then you have at your disposal the routine of: 'I'll stop the car and put you out.' The noise goes on. You stop the car and put him out of it. You wait for the noise to subside. You readmit him. Peace – in theory. It works once, maybe twice, but after that they start to enjoy it. They figure out, quite rightly, that the hell that is car journeys is because of confined space and the prolonged proximity of other humans. As this is instantly relieved by a quick spell by the side of the road while the rest of the family is still stuck in the confined space, fuming, it turns into quite a laugh. I won't patent this one.

Our car-sick child told us the other day that car-sick pills make her car-sick.

One of the biggest rows I've ever had with my wife was over whether a length of road on the map was, or was not, one centimetre long. The kids were cowering in the back as the battle raged to and fro on the front seat. We struck new heights of intelligent argument: Is. Is not. Is. Is not . . . You would think that the matter would at least have been resolved when we got home and a ruler was found. Not so. We disagreed about what bit of road it was that we had been arguing about: Is. Is not. Is. Is not . . .

Holidays at Home
Watch out here for the slow descent into hell. A week, usually half-term, may start off bright and breezy with a trip to the Planetarium or a theme park somewhere. This is not always a great success because four million other desperate parents have had the same idea. Once gigantic queues have been negotiated, the entertainment on offer, you think, was okay but a bit patronizing and the youngest one didn't understand it and spent most of the time in the toilet. The food cost more than that brilliant little meal you had at Rossi's Pizzeria the other week and this time all that was on offer was triangular-shaped bits of fried wood. The kids loved it though because they squeezed the sachets of tomato sauce, mayonnaise and brown sauce at each other. 'Hooray, we're firemen.' Blurp blurp. You arrive home tired but content. Day One covered.

Day Two you had down as: shopping, library, park and visiting the Bloomfields. Even with the kids in tow this turns out to be a surprisingly successful day. Sainsbury's survived the tantrum when you refused to buy your youngest a box of After Eights. The library now has a good stock of tapes, videos and CDs and they have allowed you back in after the little misunderstanding over custard in the Roald Dahl cassette. The park was a disaster because the older one fell in doggy-do. The problem here wasn't the smell or the mess but the hysteria. This is your fault because only last week you had warned them of the dangers of eating doggy-do. While you did this, they spent the whole time giggling, even when you told the story of the little boy who lost his sight as a result of the little beast that lays its eggs in doggy-do. At the end of the story, your children pointed out that they didn't have any desire whatsoever to eat doggy-do so it probably wouldn't crop up as a problem. You said that no one knows when you eat doggy-do, you can do it without knowing which isn't quite what you meant but by now you were so sick of the whole thing you couldn't go on talking about it. Now one of the kids with doggy-do on his coat is hysterical: 'I'm going blind. I'm going blind.' Old ladies from a mile off have spotted you as a child-abuser and are even now ringing social services. The visit to the Bloomfields was a great relief after this and you were able to share with them some of the minor problems you've had over the last few weeks like subsidence under the house, the burglary and the piles. Your friend recommends putting baby lotion on your finger and pushing it back inside (the piles, that is, not the subsidence), just as all the children walk in and say that they want to put on a show. 'Push what back inside mummy?' asks a young Bloomfield. 'The trolley inside Sainsbury's,' says your friend without blinking. The show is nice: it's called Snow White. Snow White is killed by Devil Doggy-do.

The plan for Day Three was a cookingy, paintingy, maybe-teach-them-to-play-chessy, see-what-happensy sort of day. It ended up as a kill-each-othery sort of day because one child became convinced that her cake should have been on the top shelf in the oven. When they started strangling each other, you lost your rag completely, belted the wrong one and then sent them to opposite ends of the house 'to think about what they have done and said to each other.' Find them twenty minutes later both asleep. 'Ahhh, they were tired,' you say to yourself and great globs of guilt rise up inside as you think of the lifelong damage you have done to the child you belted. You remember a belting you once got from your aunt when it wasn't you but your cousin who nicked the golden syrup. It still burns. And there's been a certain chill between you and your cousin ever since.

If drastic steps aren't taken now you are now drifting into half-term hell. Days Four and Five have to be perked up with interesting and worthwhile activities. Energy must be expended or you will be engulfed. It may have to be the leisure centre. Yes, the middle-aged body may well have to be exposed in public. It might be Walk in the Woods with Wellies On. Don't fuss, it's only a bit of rain. That's what happens in England, and always during half-term. No I'm not angry. Let's just keep moving and be glad we've got wellies. Well, *you* have, anyway. I don't mind my feet getting a bit wet . . .

It might have to be back to the library for a stash of videos. Watch out for an American film I once picked up about a boy in the Old West who adopts a baby deer, looks after it, loves it, it even sleeps with him and licks his face, but when it gets older it eats the family's crops. Will the boy be whupped? No, it's worse, much worse. The parents make the boy go out and shoot the deer. Yep. That's what happens. Your children can't believe it. They go completely crazy, sobbing, staring madly into the distance. Nothing has ever bothered them as much as this. For the next few hours they are sniffing and sobbing. You explain that the deer wasn't really shot, it was just 'pretend', but they know that. 'It's the psychic reality of the representation that's bothering us,' they say . . . or something like that. Look out for this film. It's called something like *The Sapling*, or *The Earthling* – no, *The Yearling*. That's it. Your kids will be able to sit through *Terminator* films, *Silence of the Lambs* – no problem. *The Yearling* will crack them up.

Best of luck for half-terms at home. They test your resources to the limit.

Housework

Children will assume that we are their slaves unless we do something to prove otherwise. Stereotypically, mothers slave for boys who grow up thinking that their partners should be their slaves too. In homes where there are boys *and* girls, it is still the case that girls do more cooking, cleaning and babysitting than boys. Some people think this is okay and it's how we make sure the world goes round. Some people (like me) think that it really won't do because it keeps women back and men thinking that they are entitled to treat women as their servants. So kids in my house, watch out – you're on household fatigues.

Child labour in the industrial revolution got a very bad press. People like the Earl of Shaftesbury and Charles Dickens helped to change everyone's view of childhood: that they were not expendable little machines. From there, the Victorians moved to the opposite extreme and tried to save children from all labour and created child worship. (Though it has to be said that the period of child worship didn't prevent hellish regimes in schools and workhouses, and thousands of abandoned children on the streets.) The more affluent we have become, the more we've been able to shield children from labour and hardship. It has been taken as self-evident that an entirely carefree existence must be the best way to bring up children. I don't entirely go along with this. I think there's plenty of good reasons for introducing children early to the world of work – in moderation. The best place to start is home. Children don't know that a home is a small productive unit, unless you explain it to them. Everything that goes on in a home happens because somebody does some work, whether paid for or not. We have to explain that everything that is shopped for, cooked, cleaned, prepared, washed up, gets there because somebody works for it. Most of these jobs are dull, and explaining all this to kids is even duller, but if you don't they will just hang about waiting for you to do it for them. I reckon life's too short to live in homes where only some of the people do the work. There are too many other things to enjoy and get on with. So the work should be shared out.

Jobs kids can and should do without any supervision: washing up, loading the dishwasher, sweeping up, hoovering, tidying rooms, basic gardening, cleaning surfaces, putting their dirty washing in the basket, putting their clean clothes away, laying and clearing the table, shopping, making sandwiches, putting shopping and food away, peeling potatoes, shelling peas, making salads, cleaning the car. Under supervision: using the washing machine, cooking, painting and decorating their rooms.

Some people say that asking kids to do these things is 'more trouble than it's worth', and 'it's more work getting them to do it than if I do it myself.' This is a piece of self-deception. Or is it self-flattery? It's as if we are saying, we're so good at these jobs and you're so bad at them that there isn't any point in asking you. Or at a deeper level, we don't want children to do these things because if they do they will become less dependent on us. And there's a part of us that wants children to be helpless and dependent because it makes us feel more valuable, more needed. So what sometimes happens is we put children in a double-bind:

PARENT: Would you clear the table please?

MARY: It's not my turn. I did it on Wednesday.

PARENT: George, clear the table.

GEORGE: I cleared it yesterday.

PARENT: Well, I know as sure as dammit it's not my turn. Both of you do it.

(Children start to clear the table and go more and more slowly, dribbling gravy off the edge of plates and bumping into each other. They squabble.)
PARENT: Oh I don't know why I bother asking you two. It's more trouble than it's worth. Put it down, I'll do it. In the end it's always me that has to do it, isn't it? I slave away cooking the meal, you'd have thought the least I could do was put my feet up afterwards and know that the table was being cleared . . .

So the children get to know that if they kick up a bit of a fuss they get out of it. But they also get an earful about how incompetent, dependent and immature they are. If this hypothetical parent had *left the room* saying, 'Can you two clear the table please?', and if both children knew that it was their job to get the place looking nice and if they didn't they wouldn't get the next meal, then we wouldn't need to offload a whole heap of stuff about how hard-pressed we are while intimating how much we enjoy children being dependent on us. I hate to say it, but some parents' sense of self-worth is so weak that it is only through keeping their children dependent that they can feel good about themselves. The trouble is that it doesn't feel all that good because dependent, pampered children treat their parents badly and the parents feel unloved, put upon and overworked. Getting children to work around the home is an effective way to break this vicious circle.

But what if they refuse? Of course they will refuse and drag their feet and break things. They're angry that you're not their slave in the way that you were when they were tinies. There's a part of all of us that wants to regress and be mollycoddled and it fights the part of us that wants to stand on our own two feet and manage life for ourselves. The jobs around the home often take on symbolic meaning as they come to represent services and obligations to other people. Serving someone a meal can represent affection, as can tidying someone's room or washing someone's underwear. Of course it doesn't necessarily represent the same thing to the servicer as to the serviced. Me washing your trousers may be a loving act, but you having clean, pressed trousers may be simply what you think is owing to you. When children hear you asking them to do these jobs around the house, there may be a part of them that sees this as a withdrawal of affection. That's why it's sometimes such a fight to get them to do it. We may need to reassure them that just because they are now old enough to tidy their room, doesn't mean that we don't love them any the less – in fact it helps us love them more.

And yes, they still refuse and kick up a stink. If it comes down to confrontation then we're in sanctions time. If you don't do this, then you won't get that. If you won't clean your room, you're not going to Kate's tonight. We have to just dig in, stick to deals, make reasonable, realizable threats like that and if the deal is broken stick to the sanction. She doesn't clean her room, she doesn't go to Kate's. Once my deal was that if they didn't clear up their toys I would put them all in a black bin bag and throw them out. After two hours they hadn't even begun to put their toys away so I put them in the bin bag. Ten years later they still remember the scene and remind me of it in order to prove what a sod I am. They have a song, which they sing to the tune of 'Rudolf the red-nosed reindeer', that begins: 'Dad is a turdy tyrant . . .' I was probably too tough on that occasion. Though I should say in self-defence they got all their toys back by the end of the week.

Manners

I was on a radio programme recently and the panel had to think up one thing they would revive from the past. I said London trams and trolleybuses, and a well-known agony aunt on the panel said manners. I guess there is a generally held view that children are less polite and ruder today than we were. I wonder. When we were children, adults were always telling us that we were less polite and ruder than they were when they were children. I can remember on one occasion standing with my friend Brian at the bus terminus when a hugely tall man got off the bus and we started laughing. He looked down at us and said, 'Don't they teach you manners anymore?'

I've always remembered this because I couldn't at the time think of any occasion on which someone had 'taught me manners'. Of course, teachers and parents were doing it all the time, it's just that I didn't recognize it as such. And if that tall man at the bus terminus was anything to go by, I hadn't learnt them either.

But just because we were thought of as unmannerly doesn't

mean that nothing's changed. In the post-war period children probably have, gradually, become less deferential to adults. There's no actual evidence for this. It's just something that everyone feels. If this is so, then it's not all bad. It might be tough for adults to cope with but that might be because of a mismatch of signals. We might be slowly but surely giving children more freedom, more rights to run their own lives, more opportunities to choose how they spend their time and buy the things they want, but we still want some of the old kinds of ways of being spoken to. I would guess that we can't have both. If as a society we are encouraging children to be more in control of their own lives, then we can't expect them to go on treating us deferentially.

I think we're entitled to expect from children the same level of 'manners' – courtesy, consideration, respect, or whatever other term you might use – as we would from another adult. But more than that? I suppose most of us would say, yes, because they are children. And this is the mismatch between our idea of childhood and what our children are actually like. 'Childhood' is an idea that we carry around in our heads full of pictures of children of the past, children in books, advertisements and films. We have an image of the ideal child, as if children were cars. And one of the reasons we want that ideal child is to make us, as parents, look good. The problem is that the ideal is mostly out of reach and out of touch. It's beyond most children's possible ways of behaving and it's out of touch with all the other messages we give to children about how to behave, and out of touch with the new ways of behaving that children are making for themselves.

All this means that it's hard to fix the basic rules and there are enormous variations between what one group of people thinks is acceptable and another thinks is not. Some people are amazed that in one or two of the primary schools my children have attended, the school's policy has been for the children to call teachers by their first names. What does that policy signify? I suppose it's a way of saying that teachers aren't different from your parents or their friends whom your children also know by their first names. If you know people as Mr, Mrs etc. it suggests a certain distance, formality and perhaps an implied deference *by right*. And this is a sticking point for many adults. We think that we *are* entitled to respect and deference from children by right,

without question, simply because we are adults and they are children. The first-names principle suggests that we have to *earn* respect and deference. To tell the truth it's hard work to earn the respect of children. Adults *en masse* are not necessarily particularly wise or pleasant. They don't seem to be making a brilliant job of running the world. In the past this state of affairs could be hidden from children. The adults they met, parents, teachers, churchmen and women could put on a brave show of collective wisdom and tell children that all was for the best and that progress was in hand. Wise men and women like prime ministers and monarchs were doing a damned good job on our behalf. Baden-Powell's chats to the scouts were full of these sentiments. A modern Baden-Powell couldn't get away with saying these things. The old vertical hierarchy in which people believed that the higher up the system, the wiser our leaders were, and that such people had our best interests at heart, is scarcely believed by anyone anymore. How could you, with politicians and royalty exposed as behaving no better and probably worse than the rest of us? Children know all this. They watch the news and the comedy shows that expose it all. They hear grown-ups talking about it. The air is full of disrespect, cynical laughter and mockery. Why should children be somehow immune from this? Why should they be the only ones still expected to behave in unquestioningly respectful ways?

What I am trying to say is that 'manners' isn't just a matter of what goes on behind closed doors, or even simply a matter of what parents and teachers work out as a common code of decent intercourse. 'Manners' is part of the lubricant of the whole social fabric and so is part of the whole way in which we see each other. On an everyday basis, of course, we want children to say please and thank you, not to spit at us, not to interrupt conversations as if they are the only people who matter, not to snatch things off other people, not to throw food about, not to wreck other people's possessions, not to use force on other people just in order to get what they want, to respect other people's privacy . . . and so on. But these are the 'manners' we expect of other adults. I can't really think of any code of behaviour we can fairly expect of children *simply because they are children*. One might say that as children are at the bottom end of the social learning curve, to that extent they *are* in a different situation. But there's a world of difference between on the one hand reminding children to say please and thank you because it makes everyone feel better, and on the other telling children to call adults 'sir' or to stand up when we come into the room. The first is initiating children into what everyone does, and the second is demanding that children accept inferior status. I would guess that the twentieth century has seen a slow increase in the number of people who would agree with the first and not the second, but it's by no means unanimous.

Pets

We had a cat who died. She was called Mickie and views on her were divided. I thought she was stupid and everyone else thought she was brilliant. She started to go bald and when we took her to the vet he said that she was 'over-grooming'. So he pumped her full of hormones. Then she started having chunks missing from her. Literally, a hole appeared in her armpit – well, technically speaking, legpit. We took her to the vet and he said that she was still 'over-grooming'. I started to have fantasies about how each week we would take her in and there'd be another bit missing – an ear, or a leg – and each time the vet would say, 'I know what that is: over-grooming.' In the end we would go in and all we would have left was her tail.

One day while we were talking about Mickie, my youngest, who was about four at the time, looked very closely at her and said, 'Does Mickie *know* she's a cat?' That was so deep we didn't know where to begin. Do cats know they're cats? I said they probably know they're not dogs but apart from that I couldn't be sure.

So, anyway, Mickie died. Well, she didn't die exactly, she faded away. She got weaker and weaker and we asked the children whether we ought to take her to the vet to finish her off but they were sure we shouldn't do that. No euthanasia for them. And as we didn't have the money to put her into a hospice on an opium drip, the older girl sat with Mickie as she just faded away. It was a sad and tough time for her because Mickie was originally her cat and she had had her from when they were both very young. She buried her in the garden in the middle of the lawn under a pile of dark blue quarry tiles.

Because I wasn't an enormous fan of Mickie, I was a bit reluctant about rushing out and getting a replacement. The kids were itching for another furry creature to care for but we kept talking about how they make holidays difficult, and there wasn't really room in the house for a polar bear. They weren't impressed. Resentment simmered. It became a kind of eyes-down, don't-mention-it sort of subject. Then one day while we were sitting having our tea, two cats appeared at our patio door. They looked in through the glass and said in a cheesed-off sort of way:

'Can we come in? It's really cold out here. We won't stay long, honest.'

'Go away,' I said. 'We had a cat and she died. Goodbye.'

But the kids said, 'Oh go on Dad, let them in. It's really cold outside.' So I backed down.

'OK you can come in, but you're not staying. You can just pop in for a bit, then it's out.'

So the cats came in. One was a grey-blue colour and the other was a tabby and the moment they were inside they started checking out the house.

'Nice place you've got here.'

'Nice sofa. William Morris, is it?'

Then the tabby one said, 'Sorry we haven't introduced ourselves. My name's Tigs . . .'

'And my name's Smudge,' said the grey-blue, 'named after the Arsenal centre-forward, Smudger Smith.'

'Great,' I said, 'nice to have met you, now go.'

'Oh,' says Tigs, 'look, there isn't any chance of a bite to eat, is there? We're a bit down on our luck at the moment.'

Smudge was over by the cupboard by now, sniffing at the door. 'It's OK,' she said, 'they've got stacks of cat food in here. It must have been left over from the time that dozy one conked out. Great, looks like nice stuff.'

'OK, you can have some of that but not in here.'

'That's OK,' said Tigs, 'anywhere will do us. Thanks very much. It's very nice of you. Psst, Smudge,' he said under his breath, 'don't push your luck with this guy. Just humour him, make him feel he's doing you a favour, like this: thanks a lot sir. That's very kind of you. Outside will be just fine, it's so much more hygienic, isn't it? Humans don't want to be bothered with the smell of cat food, do they? I can understand that.' So the children fed them outside and off they went.

The next day, they're back at the patio door. Same moany voices: 'Can we come in?'

'Yeah,' shout the kids, 'Smudge and Tigs are back. Brilliant! Come in, come in.'

'Thanks,' says Tigs, 'very nice of you. Look, I know we asked for this yesterday, but there isn't any chance of a bit of . . . you know . . . a quick little snack, is there?'

And almost before he can finish, the kids are rushing to get the cat food out and fork it in to a bowl. They're heading outside with the stuff when Tigs says, 'Oh look, you wouldn't mind awfully, would you, if we had our dinner inside? It's just that it *is* very cold out there.'

'Yeah,' say the kids, 'hooray, let's feed them in here.'

'OK, OK, but straight after that, it's out.'

'Of course, of course,' says Tigs.

'What do you mean, "of course"?' mutters Smudge. 'Why do you keep slimeballing your way round this lot? Don't ask, just take.'

'You shut up,' says Tigs. 'I know what I'm doing. I've done this lark before. Let me handle the buttering-up stuff. It makes them feel good, and next thing, we've got our legs under the table.'

So they get on with their dinner and when they're finished, I say, 'OK, guys, that's it. It's been great having you but time's up. Out.'

'What did I say?' says Smudge to Tigs. 'You've got nowhere with all your charm. Upstairs in these places, there's loads of comfy beds. We should have made a run for it, got upstairs and snuggled down.'

'Patience, Smudge. Watch this.'

'Look, thanks a lot for the grub, it was really nice. I can see that you're very keen that we don't hang around much longer. I understand that. No one wants a guest who outstays his welcome, but, it *is* actually very cold out there. You wouldn't really expect us to stay out there *all night* would you?'

'Yeah,' I say with menace.

'Oh no,' say the kids. 'We wouldn't want you to stay out there all night, would we? You stay. Brilliant. Tigs and Smudge.'

So the cats go over to the sofas.

'Very nice sofas. Very comfortable. Just right.'

And Smudge turns to me and says, 'Oi, squeeze up a bit, will you? You're taking up loads of room on this thing.'

So Tigs and Smudge came to stay. Sometimes they lick each other, sometimes they fight. Their preferred place to live is in empty cardboard boxes. How do we solve the holiday problem? They go to a hotel. A man called Ken calls round for them and takes them away. Tigs hasn't quite figured out that Ken is the chauffeur but the moment he appears, Smudge heads for a dark, inaccessible hole somewhere. The children spend hours interpreting what they're thinking and what their characters are like. They imitate their movements, they talk to them and speak their thoughts for them, make up stories about them . . . What a strange thing to do.

When I was a boy, we had a cat called Simpkin, named after the cat in Beatrix Potter's *The Tailor of Gloucester*. I can remember the day we got her, and I ran through the streets with her under my jacket, because we had bought her from the butcher in the High Street. We gave her Kit-e-Kat and she sicked it up so after that my mum said we had to give her whiting. She had kittens but got cancer soon afterwards. I remember lying in bed stroking her and finding this big soft swelling on her back. When we took her to the vet I was amazed and staggered that he stuck a thermometer up her bum. I remember naming all the kittens: one was called Sherpa because she was very good at climbing up the hill you made with your knees in bed. One was called Share because she had a division sign on her back. And one, my parents called Archie. This was because there was a cat called Archie in a book called *Archie and Mehitobel*. Years later I found out that there is a cat in a book called *Archie and Mehitobel* but the cat is called Mehitobel. Archie is a cockroach who writes free verse.

We kept a slow worm for a while, but it kept escaping and we would find it on the stairs all dry and fluffy. I kept pond snails and water beetles in a dark green aquarium. And the snails made spawn and these turned into more pond snails. Then I caught a fish called a loach and put it in the aquarium and everyone told me that there was no such thing as a loach. It's called a roach. I said that it was a loach and when people came to see it, we could never find it because the aquarium was so dark and green. But sometimes at night, when I was all alone in my room, it would come out of the gloom and show its face for a moment or two. I knew it was in there.

Once, my mother said that we could collect nettles in the park and bring them back and grow tortoiseshell butterflies. I thought this was incredible but she said that the little green specks on the nettle leaves were tortoiseshell butterfly eggs. They were certainly eggs because they hatched into caterpillars. Black furry ones. Every day we had to collect more nettles for them, and we kept them in an aquarium with a perforated paper lid. Then a few months later they started to make cocoons for themselves and hung themselves up from the edges of the nettle leaves. I took one and kept it in my room and sometimes the bottom bit twitched. But then it stopped twitching. It just sat in my room without doing anything. One day Dad called us in and we watched tortoiseshell butterflies crawl out of their cocoons. 'Open the window,' he said and they crept out on to the windowsill and flew away.

All these moments matter.

P.S. Have you noticed that children love pets but don't like shopping for pet food, cleaning out cages, clearing up cat poo in the corner, emptying litter trays, taking dogs for walks etc. Kids like pets so that they can practise loving. They can do it without having any of the worries that they won't be loved back, or that it will be taken the wrong way, or that it over-commits them and so on. It's like a no-strings relationship. Then along comes a parent and says things like, 'That cage needs cleaning out.' What a let down. The kid was in it for the stroking, not all that boring, smelly stuff.

A few of the brutal facts of life need to be asserted here, and a fair division of labour. Okay, so you can't necessarily expect a young child to empty the cat litter (though children in rural areas, in non-industrial countries, and in our not so distant past have all done that sort of thing and worse), but you can expect them to shovel the cat litter out of the bag into the tray or to clean the feeding bowl, line rabbit hutches and the like. If we don't, then we foster a weird idea of animals as teddy-bears. Mind you, it's a real bind trying to get them to do these things, because at heart they would prefer it if their pets were biology free, apart from their moist, adoring eyes.

Pocket Money

Pocket money for children was invented to teach children to be worthy members of a Nation of Shopkeepers. Children would learn the meaning of the words: savings, loan, debt, extortion and ruin. The key to all this would be the Money Box. The Money Box is a fetish or household god sitting quietly in the corner of your children's bedrooms waiting for its next offering. Toyshops now offer mini replicas of pirates' treasure chests or American bank safes to add a little extra thrill to the business. Your child can now spend many happy hours opening and closing these receptacles, asking you if you know how to crack the safe or plunder the chest and then showing you the little secret chamber inside.

Apart from the religious aspect of all this – introducing young children to the worship of money – there is, in theory, a practical side too: keeping money safe. I have found that there are several snags here:

1. I run short of change for the bus. Can't face the bus-conductor's face if I were to offer a twenty pound note, so I nip upstairs, lever open a money box with a screwdriver, nick a couple of quid, and leave a squalid little note saying 'I O U 2 QUID, OK? LUV DAD XXX'. This is never paid back, seeps like a running sore for years and is remembered at moments such as weddings and funerals. 'Don't you remember Dad how when I was four you once stole two quid off me and you promised to pay me back but you never did? Don't you remember, Dad?'

2. Older children pick up these bad habits from you and go on similar raids when they are short of money for make-up,

tickets for football matches and protection money for class bullies. This leads to massive family rows which begin with your youngest child saying quietly: 'I thought I had fifty-two pee in here . . .'

You say calmly, 'Oh, you must have spent it on Smarties.'

'No,' she says, 'I think Dave's nicked it.'

This results in the following heartwarming scene:

YOU: Come here Dave. (*Enter Dave, shiftily*) Did you nick Sarah's money?

DAVE: (*Shiftily*) Why do you believe everything she says? You're always picking on me. It doesn't matter what I say, you only believe what she says. Nothing's fair round here. You wouldn't care if I fell under a bus. This place makes me sick. I'm going to ring Childline.

YOU: Yes, I know all that, but did you nick any money out of Sarah's money box?

DAVE: (*Shifty silence*)

YOU: I'm going to take that silence as meaning, yes, you did nick the money.

DAVE: (*Continued shifty silence*)

You now have several days of discussion in which you try to find out exactly why Dave needed to nick the money. Couldn't he have come and asked you for it? Couldn't he have 'talked the whole thing through'? Couldn't he have got by with what he's got? As for the little one, you will notice that she has begun to ask some very shrewd questions about the safety of the family cash in the bank account and why do you believe the mortgage people when they say that they are putting your money somewhere safe to buy the house. You begin boldly by talking about friendly building societies and honesty and end up as a muddled wreck convinced that sleazy international mafiosi currency fiddlers are after your home.

3. Your child loses the key to his money box. This always happens just as you're about to leave the house for somewhere where delightful goodies are available for him to spend his money on. 'Don't worry, darling, I'll lend you the money and when we find the key, you can pay me back.' This is nonsense. The money in your wallet isn't the same as the money in his money

box. It's not as nice. It hasn't got his name on. Outings to places like the Transport Museum or an open farm can be wrecked simply because the key to the money box can't be found and your fiver doesn't look like his fiver.

4. Your child loses the money box. Ho ho, you're thinking. A Rosen exaggeration here. Not so. One of mine lost his money box. It was 12″ × 5″ × 3″, bright red and clanked loudly when picked up. We knew for certain that it hadn't left the house. How can you lose something like that? It was full of treasure: several birthday fivers, four pfennigs, a franc, a nickel, an Australian dollar, an exciting amount of lira and a very hard conker. It stayed lost until Christmas. Santa staggered down the chimney with a massive grey and red replica of a US high security safe, with special combination locking system and thoughtfully packed with pfennigs, nickels, Australian dollars, millions of lira and old conkers. The child was appeased. The potentially jealous sister was given a money box designed and disguised as a big red book with the words, 'A Big Book of Poems by A. Wordsmith' on the cover. All was peace. Then the old money box turned up. For safekeeping away from Mike 'Screwdriver' Rosen it had been stuffed into a moonboot and dumped in the bottom of the dressing-up bin. As both moon-booting and dressing-up had been overtaken by Nintendo and *The Beano* the money box had lost all chance of being discovered months earlier.

All this fandango leaves the matter of pocket money itself untackled. This is because I, along with many other parents I meet, am a failed pocket-money provider. My mother was brilliant. Each week she would give my brother and me our dues. As he was four years older than me, he got a slice more but I could always look forward to getting his level of pay when I was his age. I can remember when my rate was a thruppenny bit. So I saved my thruppenny bits till I could afford to buy a toy car, (weren't the 1950s wonderful, we knew what it meant to save and prosper then, didn't we?) and I lived happily ever after. Er – well, actually no. I confess here for the first time that I nicked money out of my mother's purse to get enough money to buy a railway carriage for our model railway and I went on a shoplifting spree to Woolworth's to get a push-and-go racing car. This is a round-about way of saying that I don't really buy the line that the little-by-little, on-the-dot, on-the-day pocket-money principle is a training in money management, honesty, thrift and responsibility. It may be for some people but it's not necessarily so.

So after several false starts pocket money for my children has died the death. In its place we have the muddle-through. This means that the children's own money comes variously from relatives at birthdays and Christmas, mothers, fathers or step-parents when their imaginations run low at birthdays and Christmas, lump sums at the start of outings or holidays, payment for large laborious favours performed for grateful parents, and *on negotiated demand*. This last source of loot seems only to affect the over-elevens as they start to go off to the cinema or the leisure centre on their own and it means that you can keep an eye on amounts going in and out. I've tried to work to the principle of Careful Generosity.

'Yes, you can have money to go to the cinema this weekend but not the cinema *and* Arsenal.'

'But Shirley's going to both.'

'That's because Shirley's Dad is giving her guilt money to make up for the fact that he's not going to be around for the weekend.'

The Careful Generosity principle is also useful when you're broke. Instead of having to run through the 'money doesn't grow on trees' routine, you now simply say, 'Sorry, you can't go ice skating. I'm skint. I'm cutting back by not buying the Sunday papers; you're cutting back by not going ice skating.' After all, somewhere along the line you want your children to cotton on to the idea that money comes in as a result of work, nearly everything costs money and only royalty, stars, big business execs and fraudsters can afford to buy whatever they want. This is where the laborious favours come in, for example, cleaning the car, chopping up the Christmas tree . . . but not, in our house anyway, for ordinary household duties like shopping, hoovering and room tidying. If you pay them for everything then it misses the point. Clearing up the mess of everyday living is a thankless, unpaid but essential job. Rendering other people a service is worth a bob or two.

Reading

Question: Why doesn't my son read books? Question: Why does my daughter only read horror books? Question: Why don't they do good books like *Wind in the Willows* at school anymore? Question: Am I right in banning my children from reading Enid Blyton and comics? Question: Should I stop them watching TV to make them read more? Question: Where can I get advice about good books for children?

I often hear these kinds of questions and they all speak of the same thing: a worry that children are falling behind. When children start to read, what they read and don't read seems to worry us perhaps more than anything else – with the possible exception of writing. Fair enough, some will say, as reading is the key to everything else. It may be, but not if we take 'reading' to mean something very simple and mechanical.

We use the word 'reading' to mean a lot of different things. 'Reading' can mean being able to read out loud a page of writing. 'Oh, she can read,' we say when we hear a child reading out loud. But I can read German books out loud without understanding more than about ten per cent. Am I reading? When we get excited that our child is reading because she can say all the words in front of her, can we be sure it's worth getting excited about? Maybe yes, maybe no. A child who is able to read is not necessarily a child who can understand what she's reading, nor is she necessarily a child who chooses to read or wants to read. Anyone who has worked with children knows that there are thousands of children who are like this.

This means that the business of teaching reading has to include the idea of encouraging children to want to read, and to *choose* to read. So whatever method is used to help children arrive at understanding that the black and white squiggles on a page signify words and sentences, needs to include some of the things that make reading pleasurable for that particular child, at that particular moment and at that particular age. Otherwise, why bother to learn to read? This means that we have to find things that a child finds interesting, enjoyable and worth reading. For many children the problem with reading isn't that it's too difficult but that it's either dull or irrelevant. Put it this way, you or I try to avoid reading anything that is dull or irrelevant – children will try and do just the same.

So the first principle as parents – rather than teachers – is to find as many ways as possible to make reading interesting and enjoyable. It may well be up to us, just as much as for teachers, to prove to our children that reading is worth the effort. Do you give off the vibe that *you* enjoy reading? Do you talk about the things that you read? Do you share what you're reading with the rest of the family, by mentioning something interesting in the paper or talking about a novel that made you think this or that? Before you make any complaints about your child or his or her teacher, think about whether your child has a model from you that reading is good fun and worthwhile. A couple of my kids are mad about football. They wouldn't be seen dead reading the broadsheet newspapers, until recently when I started reading out the extra dirt that was being dished up in the sports columns in the heavies!

The next question to ask of yourself is: do you find ways to make connections between what's in books and what's going on in everyday life? My step-daughter was 'doing' the Tudors and Stuarts at school. She began to get interested in the topic. An exciting children's novel set in this period is *Cue for Treason* by Geoffrey Trease. Suddenly this book became desirable, and she was able to feed into her reading some of the excitement she was getting from the topic at school. If you go to a museum, a farm or a castle, you might find that one moment will grab your child's interest. Go with it. Find something while the interest is still there that will nourish it – a game, a spotter's book, a story. You might find Steven Biesty's book that is a cross-section of a castle or discover a poster of different kinds of farm animals and the like. If your child is keen on a particular sport or any TV programme, you can find a book or annual that is tied in with it. If your child is supposed to be reading a book at school and is finding it heavy going, see if there's some kind of activity that might help it come to life: a video of the book?

It's quite possible that somewhere along the line your child will lose sight of the fun of sharing books with people. The great thing about TV is that you can often talk about what you've seen with someone else within a day or so. Books don't always offer this. This means that to keep the interest going it might be a good idea for you to read what the child is reading and listen to what your child has got to say about the book. You may think the book isn't up to much. Be very careful about dismissing it or you'll make the child seem small for enjoying it. Any activities that you do with your children – dress-making, gardening, football, going to the cinema – you can find books that tie in with that activity: talk about them, share them and above all, leave them lying around.

If all this is going on, your child will be finding out some other meanings of the word 'reading', like when we say that someone can 'read' what's going on in a meeting, or in a game. It means 'figure out' or 'interpret'. When we read a book, we don't just take in one word, one meaning at a time. As we read, we run ahead of ourselves, we guess what's coming next, and at the same time we hold in our heads what we've just read. Quite a lot of the time we have to re-read to make sure we've fully understood what is being said. Quite often we try to get behind what is being said to a deeper, unspoken meaning. We're trying to 'read the game', figure out what's really going on. On a simple level, we do this when we read a whodunit. For children to learn how to really read they need plenty of practice at different kinds of books, plenty of practice at talking about books, what they mean and how they might be written differently, or could have turned out differently. In so doing, children also discover something else about reading: that a book, any book, doesn't just mean one thing. There isn't only one opinion about a character, or even about the way an aeroplane or a fox is described in an encyclopedia. Reading also means coming up with different versions. We might say in life: 'His reading of the situation is that she's very unhappy, but I think she is very worried.' A 'reading' is a version. When children get a chance to say what their reading of a book is, their version, they can get very animated and excited about it. That's a good feeling for a child to have and will only make them want to read more. It's possible that school won't offer that so it may be something that you can do at home. All books are there to be argued with.

So far I've treated reading as if it's obviously and naturally a vitally important thing to do. It's obvious (though perhaps not natural) that I would think this way as I make my living writing and spend many, many hours reading. But even someone as prejudiced as me can see that many people get by in life without reading *books*. They read newspapers, magazines, reports, letters, posters, tax claims, manuals, instructions, computer programmes . . . but not books. Such people are not inferior, more likely to treat their friends and lovers badly, more likely to rob old ladies or bash people over the head. And conversely, plenty of avid book readers have been unbelievably horrible to friends or to anyone they regard as inferior. Trying to con children into believing that reading makes you a better person should be forgotten. Let's be honest. All we can say about a child who reads a wide range of different books is that it will make school subjects and passing exams easier. This may or may not lead them into getting a better job and may or may not make them happier or wealthier. I would like to think that if you constantly help your child argue with what is written in books, and enjoy discovering that one can have opinions about what's being read, your child will also enjoy questioning what's being told him or her by the main outlets of opinion: TV, newspapers, radio and political statements.

But what about those questions I asked earlier?

Why doesn't my son read books?
I used to say this. Then I discovered that thousands if not millions of parents were going about saying it too. I also discovered that though these millions of boys were not reading novels they were reading plenty of other things. Now it may be a cause of the odd bout of sadness that my sons stopped reading stories and novels when they were twelve but it's quite another thing to say they aren't reading anything at all. They read skateboard magazines, joke books, TV comedy show tie-ins, 'amazing phenomena' books like the *Guiness Book of Records*, *The World's Most Amazing*

. . . (freaks, murders etc.), football fanzines, computer magazines, newspapers, comics, graphic novels and so on. They have explained to me why they aren't interested in reading novels: they take too long to set everything up, telling you what people look like and what they're thinking. Novels are often about uninteresting things like love and marriage and divorce. Novels are often set in uninteresting places like anytime in the past, the countryside, any other country other than America. (See what barbarians I have brought up.)

Clearly they are affected by what's hip and cool in the way of cinematic and visual media. They're saying they want action not description or psychology, they want it modern, English speaking and non-domestic. To this, teachers might well say tough! You're going to hear of something else of the world apart from what's on offer down at your local video store. But parents don't have to be teachers. And there's always the middle ground: finding books that they won't find at school, for instance. There are a few authors trying to say interesting things to children, especially boys, in modern, cinematic ways of writing. Try Paul Jennings, Morris Gleitzmann and, for older children, Robert Cormier.

Why does my daughter only read horror books?
The simple answer is because all the other girls are. The author and critic Edward Blishen once said to me that the best way to get children reading and to keep them at it, is if the habit spreads like contagion or the plague. He meant that children will long to read when they start telling each other about what a good read this or that book is. A few years ago ten-year-old girls were telling each other that Judy Blume was a must: her books were funny, sexy, sad, thoughtful and 'realistic'. They had to be read. Now the girls are passing horror books to each other, testing out just how brave they can be in coping with murders, ghosts, vampires, monsters and the like. I have seen parents wilt with dismay at the craze. Before wilting I would urge you to have a read of one of them yourself. In fact, many of these so-called horror books aren't very horrific at all. Some kind of danger or unpleasantness threatens to engulf the group (mostly teenage) but then everything is resolved in some rational and highly moral way. Authors like R.L. Stine and Christopher Pike know very well that they have a young

audience who are interested in how and why teenagers become, stay or stop being friends. The horror element is merely a thrilling coating to what is at heart a 'realistic' saga about say, teasing, bullying, first sex, self-doubt and the like. All the ones I have read finish up with some worthy sentiment like: this wouldn't have happened if you had listened to what your best friend was going through instead of ignoring her and trying to ingratiate yourself with that beautiful but vain newcomer. The books you may have read as a child are not necessarily superior to these moral, if grisly, tales.

Why don't they do good books like *Wind in the Willows* at school anymore?

There is a whole raft of books that used to be on the middle-class parent's list of recommended reading. When the National Curriculum flirted with the idea of laying down rules about what children should read, a list of 'children's classics' was compiled. One of the reasons why many schools aren't keen on doing these books any more is because quite a few of them have obnoxious and horrible passages. What can he possibly mean by this, you might be wondering. You may have forgotten the passages in *Peter Pan* where James Barrie talks about mothers, or kissing. You may have forgotten the piper at the gates of dawn in *Wind in the Willows*, Injun Joe and the 'nigger' Jim in Mark Twain's books or Richmal Crompton's sneers at the Irish in *Just William*. Don't get me wrong, I am not saying that these books are bad or not worth reading. I am simply explaining one of the reasons why teachers choose to avoid these books today. They ask themselves, is it worth the time and energy to discuss these passages with young children? Are the 'classics' so much better than modern books or do we read them out of habit and nostalgia?

When we call a book a classic we tend not to ask whether it is any good or not. Instead, we simply invite other people, especially children, to sit back and admire. I don't think any book merits that alone. In fact when you look closely at 'children's classics' there can be all sorts of dubious meanings there. After all, what precisely is *Wind in the Willows* about? A group of middle-class English bachelors try to whip a wayward aristocrat into line so that he can resume his role as squire. If he doesn't shape up, the riotous and dangerous masses might take over. Hmmmm. *Peter Pan*: if women always behaved like doting mothers, boys wouldn't want to run away and, thank god, wouldn't want to grow up and have to be married to women who are not their mothers. Hmmmm. These are only my 'readings' and there are plenty of others but perhaps they will serve as reminders that no text is sacred and *has* to be read. Not even as part of the heritage industry.

Am I right in banning my children from reading Enid Blyton and comics?

No. Several of my children have read and enjoyed these. They've used such literature as a staging post. My step-daughter read twenty or more Blytons before she found out that 'they're all the same', and went about doing parodies of Blyton stories. If I had stopped her reading these, maybe she would never have learnt that stories are structures, shapes and patterns imposed on events and characters. She has now absorbed into her memory of stories how a whodunit works. Now she can read books that play with these memories and expectations in the knowledge that she, as a reader, will be able to make knowledgeable guesses about what's going on. She becomes a more sophisticated reader for having read Blyton.

As it happens, I am not someone who thinks that Blyton is totally and unutterably awful. I read *Malory Towers* not long ago and I thought that it handled the ways in which a group of girls get to know each other and jockey for position with each other quite well. The only thing I found myself choking on was the way Blyton found it necessary to keep reminding her reader what was going on and what the moral was: 'And didn't that serve her right?'

As for comics, the ones for younger readers (*The Beano, The Dandy* and the like) remain the last refuge for unpunished naughtiness. Those of us writing books often find ourselves obeying the old code that cheats must never prosper, that naughtiness will lead to a sticky end, and goodness is good. Though I would defend the idea that children's books should aim to promote ethical behaviour, comics provide a great release with their breaking of taboos. In a way, we are right to be afraid of them. They give

children all kinds of vengeful fantasies about grown-ups and dreams of impossible feats. Better by far to join in the fun than ban them. Argue with them. Say they are unfair to grown-ups and we ought to have a say. It'll keep that reading brain working, at any rate.

Should I stop them watching TV to make them read more?
This won't make them read more and will simply mark them out as freaks amongst their friends. They will either lie and pretend they have seen the programmes that their friends are talking

about, or they will repeat what you have said against TV and appear to their peers as snobs and spoilsports. Don't put them through it. Instead, you can use TV as a great stimulus to reading. Pick up on items and programmes they have found interesting and support this with written material, for example on bears, space, the novel that a series has been based on, autobiographies of stars and so on. It works the other way too. Things crop up in books that can be verified or questioned from knowledge gleaned from TV. We live in a world where television, books, films, plays, dances, computer games all refer to each other. It is, as is sometimes said, an 'inter-mediate' world. You don't gain anything by trying to chop one limb off. You just make it harder for children to pick up on what's going on.

Where can I get advice about good books for children?

Your local library, no matter how understaffed and underfunded, is still the best resource you have. Get to know the librarians, ask them for advice, ask them for addresses of the local Children's Book Group, ask them for information on authors' visits and book festivals. Take your children to see authors and book festivals even if it means travelling fifty miles. They will never forget it.

You can get together with a group of parents at your children's school and help the school to set up a school bookshop. If the school runs a book week, you can help organize it, or even initiate one. New information on children's books is available from the Young Book Trust, BBC Radio 4's *Treasure Islands*, the magazine *Books for Keeps*, and book clubs such as Letterbox Library, The Red House and Books for Your Children. If you are in a town that has a big bookshop, go in and browse through the children's books. When you're there with your child, don't shout at her to leave the books alone, something I often hear parents doing. Ask them to be careful with the books, encourage them to look at the cover, read the back, read the first page, look at the pictures and if it looks interesting, buy it. Alternatively, order it at the library.

I never overlook second-hand bookshops, jumble sales and Oxfam shops. Old comic annuals and quite recent paperbacks are usually on sale and occasionally – the treasure for me – that book I had as a child. I start raving about it, I get all misty-eyed about how I loved the little grey rabbit or the little green men, my children say that they think I'm daft but quietly it all helps to keep the flame of book-interest burning. Suddenly you might find, like one of mine, they start collecting old joke books, Thelwell cartoon books or old annuals. Ahah, you've got 'em hooked.

I have a few regrets about my children and books. One of them is that I haven't read to them as much or for as long as my parents read to me. With the younger ones especially I stopped reading to them when they were about five as they seemed to be doing plenty of reading themselves. But that misses the point. Reading can be both private *and* social and one feeds into the other. I remember my father reading us *Great Expectations*. His rendering of Trabb's boy mocking Pip's airs and graces by walking up and down the street calling out 'Don't know yer!' entered family folklore. Whenever anyone tried on a bit of snobbery we would all call out 'Don't know yer!' – a humane moment in a great book thus had a resonance we could all share, repeat and use in appropriate moments in our lives. It was this kind of thing that turned me on to reading, and perhaps I haven't been as good at doing that with my children. Perhaps I am too afraid of boring them or being laughed at for being an old book bore!

Rows

Which kinds of rows are the worst? The ones you have with your partner, the ones you have with your children, or the ones they have with each other? What a choice!

I'm sure there used to be a law against parents rowing with each other in front of children. Or there was some kind of Neighbourhood Watch Scheme: if you felt a row coming on, you'd stop yourself in case the neighbours called the cops in. I remember my parents having rows but I don't remember what they were about. I guess this is because what strikes a child most is less the subject of the argument than the plain fact that parents are arguing. And as a child you start to recognize the different styles. My mum used to have a kind of wind-up method. That is winding herself up, not someone else. She would pitch in at a low-level monotone which wasn't immediately obvious as the beginning of a row apart from a giveaway frown. The next clue that this was the business would be that the monologue could not be interrupted. Trying to distract her or pointing out minor errors of fact were useless. The monotone would turn into more of a wave shape, a rising and falling, and unanswerable questions would fly out: 'Why is it that you never do what I say?' Near the end she might bang something, bringing it down very hard on the table top. A fork or a hand. More upsetting – and very rarely – it might end in tears. Hers. And everyone would go very quiet. My dad, on the other hand, went in for mockery. His arms would start pumping out and he'd often end sequences with the words, 'Mad. Completely mad.' Sometimes, when my parents were rowing, they would both talk at the same time and so all you'd hear would be: 'I don't know why you –' 'Mad. Completely –' 'Why is it that you can't –' 'Mad, I tell you, mad.' I don't know, I really don't –' 'Utterly mad.'

One masterblaster of a row I've had in recent years took place just outside Witney in Oxfordshire. Seven of us were jammed into the car – I mean 'people-carrier' – on our way to see some Australian friends who were renting a house. The kids were beginning to get sticky: 'Are we nearly there?', 'I wanna drink', 'He's got my book.' And then I took a wrong turning. Or did I? And if I did, was it my fault? How can I drive and navigate at the same time? You've got the map. I can't read the map as I'm driving along, can I? No, I am not driving too fast. The roads don't come up on us, we come up on them. And they're all on the map. All of them.

The kids went quiet.

It's no use telling me I should have taken the turn. Sure I should have taken the turn but I didn't because you didn't tell me to. How was I supposed to know that I should have taken the turn? I know it said Witney. You thought I should take the turn because it said Witney and I thought I shouldn't take the turn because you didn't say to take it. Now you're telling me that we're heading for Birmingham because *I* didn't take the turn. It wasn't me that didn't take the turn. It was you that didn't take the turn. And now we're going to Birmingham. You drive. I'm not driving anymore. That's it. I'm stopping the car. You drive. I'm getting out the car. We'll swap seats. I'm coming round your side. I'll navigate and I'll say, 'Take the turn!' when you have to take the turn. No, I'm not driving anymore. That's it.

The kids realized by now that Dad had lost it. 'Get back in the car, Dad. You're going crazy. You took too many pills today.' (This is a cruel reference to the fact that I have no thyroid gland and take pills to compensate.) The Witney row has gone down in the family annals and is brought out as an example of how even a simple thing like driving from A to B can be made complicated by adults.

I suppose the reason why rows between couples in families are so fraught is that they are often about eleven different things at the same time. So a row about whether it was Cary Grant or Tony Curtis in *Some Like It Hot* is really about all kinds of unspoken things like: you never give me credit for knowing anything. You think I'm stupid. I think you're stupid. You don't listen to anything I say. You don't ask me what I want when we're in bed. When was the last time we went out together? You don't like the same movies as I do. You don't like anything I like. You're more interested in films than you are in me.

Children listen to us getting angrier and angrier as we shout, 'I know it was Cary Grant because of the way he spoke.' 'What you're remembering is that Tony Curtis was trying to imitate Cary Grant.' And they can't figure out what's the big deal here. Why are they getting so steamed up about an old movie?

Rather than thinking that rows between parents in front of children are directly harmful to children, it's probably more useful to think of them as pattern-setting. It's one of the key ways in which children learn about power in relationships. Rows reveal how people use and abuse power, how they try to get more of it, how people give in to others, try to reclaim it and so on. It's also a strong indicator for children as to how they might, can, should or should not behave with someone of the opposite sex. To put it crudely, a girl seeing her mother capitulate to her father's demands and bullying will absorb that as a permanent reference point for the rest of her life. She might accept, reject or adapt it, but it will dominate her views on adult relationships. No matter how many films we watch, books we read, or other life stories we hear about, the parental set-up is central in our mind. In fact, I would go as far as to argue that what parents *say* about what are right and wrong ways to treat people is much less important than what the children observe and feel about the ways in which parents actually treat each other.

Some post-sixties parents are finding to their horror that though they are stressing the importance of female economic independence, they find their daughters coming up with all sorts of 'Some-day-my-prince-will-come' type ideas. I've sometimes heard myself, in rows, repeating things my father said, (or to be more accurate, things I have *chosen* to remember and *think* I remember my father saying). I've heard myself saying or about to say, in a row, that my partner wasn't so much wrong as mad. I must have absorbed a pattern in my parents' behaviour, taken something that suited me, sided with the person of my own sex, and then come up with it in a similar situation years later. And it was all about power, a way of not arguing the case but diminishing the right of the other person to put it in the first place. There is much for children to mull on as they watch us rowing – and they can mull on it for the rest of their lives. As I've said elsewhere, part of being a parent is also being a child. The state of parenthood is a constant toing and froing in our mind, consciously or not, between thinking about how we were treated as a child and how we are treating our own children. Memories of parental rows are a fine case in point.

Likewise when you row with your children. What are these mostly about? That our children aren't turning out the way we would like them to. This means that rows between parents and children are not really like most rows between adults. Most of us behave as if parenting is a matter of trying to shape a young human being into an adult that we would approve of. We see children's behaviour as a consequence of what we have tried to tell them to do. If they behave badly this shames us. We feel responsible. This sets up very contradictory feelings in me. On the one hand I am someone who doesn't see children's feelings and thoughts as incomplete or undeveloped. Rather, they are the thought-out, complete feelings of a human being at that particular point in their lives. They aren't half feelings or small feelings. But I'm also painfully aware that the way I behave towards my children, and indeed some of the things I have said in this book, are often about managing, supervising and trying to modify children's behaviour. Can I resolve this contradiction?

Only partly. And that is by recognizing its existence, being open about it, sharing it with children, trying to give children real choices about their lives, being prepared to listen to their wishes and desires, trying to encourage an 'everyone's-entitled-to-their-say' approach. And, yes, admitting that this is in some ways a phoney democracy because the final say in what goes on is nearly always with the parents.

But back to behaviour modification – what parental rows with children are really about. Are they all necessary? Is rowing the way to get what you want anyway? Take an imaginary example. Your daughter (aged nine or so) starts having nose bleeds. You follow the latest medical advice and suggest pinching the nose just below the bone and holding it for a few minutes. You start to question her about when this happens and try to figure out if there is any common factor: overheating, sudden changes of blood pressure? You can't find any common factor. You take her to the doctor and she questions her very closely, looks up her nose, asks her if she picks her nose. No, she doesn't. The doctor is stumped. You go to an alternative medicine practitioner who suggests that it might be a deficiency in her diet or an inability to metabolize something. You follow his advice and still the nose bleeds go on.

Then one day you are sitting at the table and you notice blood on the end of her forefinger. You say, 'How did that get there?' She colours and says that she doesn't know or that maybe it got there when her nose was bleeding. The temperature is rising. You are scanning back through the hours you've spent talking about what the problem might be, thinking about it, visiting doctors, worrying. It is now beginning to look very much like a case of nose-picking. You ask what did she think she was doing sticking her finger up her nose when it was bleeding when you'd agreed that the best thing to do was to pinch the nose just above the bone. She says she was doing that anyway. You say that you don't get blood on the end of your forefinger and under the nail from pinching your nose. You only get blood like that if you stick your finger up your nose. You are now shouting.

You eventually simmer down and accept (kind of) her assurances that no, she hasn't been picking her nose all this time in order to cause nose bleeds and though she might have been doing a bit of probing this time, it wouldn't happen again. A few days later you spot it again. And this time you go spare. You start yelling, you tell her she's a liar, that she doesn't care about wasting everyone's time, disrupting everyone's lives. She starts crying, you start yelling even louder. Next time she has a nose bleed you will assume it is because she has picked her nose to cause it and it's her problem from now on. End of row. The nose bleeds stop. A year in the life of a bleeding nose comes to an end.

One of the main reasons why you have had a row rather than a quiet sit-down chat is because you are angry that you reckon your child has tried – no, succeeded in – manipulating you and an ever-widening circle of adults. In fact you are appalled that she did it, worried that she might go on through life being like this, ashamed that it's one of yours that did it. You say all this and you say that you feel that she has treated you with a complete lack of respect. You say you are not trying to be Sigmund Freud but presumably she must have been doing it to make some kind of a point: 'I want to be noticed' or 'look at me' but why the hell couldn't she have done it by saying, 'Look at me!' This is not some damned workhouse here. People can say that they are fed up about the way they are being treated. We keep saying to the children, 'Say what you think. If there's something bothering you, tell us.' Instead we get her sticking her finger up her nose and we spend hours and hours dealing with it like it's some medical problem.

The row is like a crash at a crossroads. A set of different agendas have met: her wish to be noticed, her wish to manipulate more powerful people than herself, your worry about her health, your anger at being manipulated, your anger at the waste of time, your anger at her ability to disrupt the lives of those around her, your shame that she could do this, your anxiety that she is going to be like this for the rest of her life.

Does the row solve any of this? Perhaps, perhaps not. Well, one bit of behaviour modification that works, and jolly well too, is that she has stopped making her nose bleed. She realizes that the manipulation worked, yet the last thing that a manipulator wants is for you to suss out what is going on, or even worse, for you stop allowing yourself to be manipulated. In other words a second piece of behaviour modification may have begun: it might have succeeded in reducing the extent to which she tries to manipulate you. Other people as well? Maybe, maybe not. But has the row encouraged her to do the alternative, which is to be straight and clear with people when she had needs and desires? 'I feel lonely' or, 'I wish someone would take notice of me' and the like. Probably not. Yes, you may have *said* this is preferable but did you every really hear from her what she was bothered about? No, but then you're sick and tired of asking her what she's feeling because she always says, 'Nothing. I don't know. Nothing.' So though it would indeed be preferable that she was open and not devious, not much progress is being made here. At least you were open with your feelings and she might pick up the message from that. Might. Your feelings of shame, if not despair, that you have produced and are producing someone who you feel is not up to scratch and is going to treat other people badly, (and, who knows, you might be blamed for) is untouched. But at least you didn't bottle up your feelings and try to get back at her by being equally devious and manipulative. At least you tried to break the cycle. Phew!

Rows like this make the rows that children have with each other seem like a relief – for a bit. Then the slow, persistent whining, the sharp sound of backstabbing, the steady slide into fisticuffs start to send you spare.

Doing a book signing has very little to recommend it. You sit at a table and write your name many times and then you go home. However, it can give you brief but wicked insights into family dynamics. I remember on one occasion a family was getting nearer and nearer in the queue and I started to hear the happy sound of bickering: 'No, you give him that book and I'll give this book', 'I want that book', 'But I got it first.' They were still at it by the time they got to me; the parents seemed to be ignoring what was going on between the two children. I looked at them and then at the children and the mum said, 'Oh don't worry about them, they argue all the time. It's just something they need to do.'

I was quite struck by that. Now it could be that those two boys have grown up to be psychopaths but on the other hand it may well be that it's through all their seemingly daft disputes that they were exploring all kinds of things: learning how to stick up for yourself, how to mark out your territory so that other people don't invade it, and so on. Of course as parents eavesdropping these spats, we start to listen for patterns. We might hear that one child is always getting her own way, or that one child is always provoking the argument and then whacking his opponent. That's usually when we think we have to intervene: to protect one, 'to make things fair.' I would guess that mostly, when we do this, it makes matters worse. We dive in to even things up and this merely sets up new areas for dispute: 'You always side with him', 'You always say I'm wrong', 'Just because she's the youngest doesn't mean that she didn't start it.'

Perhaps, rather than the diving-in approach, it might be more useful if we were to offer children strategies for resolving disputes by themselves. Take computers. If nothing else, they are a

fertile source for the most vicious rows. Huge claims are made by one kid against another for having hogged the computer 'for a week.' Short of standing over them like some football referee, what intervention by a parent is useful here? Yelling at them to shut up? Banning them from the computer till they shape up and get on with each other? Probably neither of these is really much good. What we did in our house was give the children a small clock to keep by the computer and to use it to give each other equal times on the thing. Of course it doesn't resolve everything, and there are plenty of exciting new areas of dispute like whether 'twenty minutes on the computer when I was round at Sandra's' should count or not. But as a principle, I think it's right: strategies for dispute-solving that they can use on other occasions as well.

This is not to deny that children's arguments are frequently about much more than the immediate issue in hand. Hence, dispute-solving strategies might sometimes (always?) be deflections from dealing with issues like: 'You used to look up to me as your older brother and now you think you know it all', or, 'I'm fed up with the way you boss me about. Just because you're older than me doesn't mean you can rule my life.' All disputes are about more than they seem but then we do have to get on with the apparatus of life. I mean by this, that we *can* stop what we are doing and investigate the deeper meaning of a row but sometimes it is better just to get on with life, and in so doing, we might find that the underlying and real reasons for a dispute ebb away. So if the row about the computer was, at a deeper level, about the older child resenting the way that the younger child had become cocky and now seemed to know it all, then, yes, it *is* possible that some of this could be resolved by bringing it all out into the open. But then it might also be resolved by the two children having a strategy that leads them to *doing* something together in an equal way. It is in the *doing* that the older child is forced to change his attitude and accept that the younger child is an equal.

Sex Education

In spite of the government's efforts to stop your child getting some sex education in school, most schools do offer it both at primary and at secondary level. Meanwhile, children tell each other all sorts of things about sex. As we all know, thinking back to when we were children, these may or may not have much to do with reality. In the playground I gathered that babies were born from between a woman's breasts and people had intercourse kneeling in front of each other. The other source of information about sex for children is movies, which are quite good at showing a lot of sighing and rolling around but not very good at showing what goes where and what happens next.

The simplest and most obvious way of tackling sex ed. is to sit down with children and start talking. 'I want to tell you about sex' is a good beginning. Books are an even better way to do it because 1) there are pictures, 2) they remember most of it, 3) they tell you things you didn't know yourself, 4) a lot of new ones are funny, 5) you can leave them with children to pore over and talk about amongst themselves. Local libraries, specialist children's bookshops, book clubs and some of the children's book departments in the big book stores will have a selection. It's quite important to get hold of a few so that you and the children can compare notes.

As a solid rule, I would argue that every question a child asks about sex has to be answered as openly and straightforwardly as possible. If you don't know the answer, then say so and suggest that you look it up in a book together. Some of the questions that children ask are in fact quite hard to answer, like: why do women have periods and men don't? How does the body know that a period should always come every 28 days? Who tells it to do it? Where did AIDS come from? What's in my testicles? and so on.

There's a big deal about the terms we use. My own feeling is that we can use the colloquial as well as the Latin terms. Words such as: willy, fanny, balls and the like aren't dirty or wrong. They are good words in certain contexts, such as in the playground, at home and between friends. There has to be a little discussion about when to use what kind of word but at the end of the day, it's the same as saying 'biccy' at home and 'biscuits' when one is being official, like labelling the shelf in supermarkets. It's one of the features of current English that familiar, slang and 'rude' words are now much more widespread than at any time since the Reformation. The word 'willy' is no big deal any more. My children find it funny when I use words that I learnt at school that aren't used much anymore, like 'goolies'.

Children will want to explore their own bodies and as brothers, sisters and friends they will design games so that they can explore each others'. This has horrified generations of parents for all kinds of reasons. For some it explodes ideas about children being 'innocent'; they find it impossible to carry in their heads the idea of childish innocence coinciding with a knowledge about sex. For some it brings up their own unresolved feelings of shame and worry about sex and so, without necessarily meaning to, they put the same worry and shame on to their children. For some there is a worry that when little boys and girls play with each other it becomes a form of abuse, that patterns of domination and even rape are laid down through these kinds of early games.

All this needs quite careful thinking about. How do we tread a path that avoids shame and guilt, doesn't dampen curiosity and safeguards children against sexual bullying? The following may sound like a cop-out, but we really have to take these as they arise. So it may be that a little boy will try to bully a little girl to 'show him hers' and that this will constitute a sexual assault. But many of us know that girls say just the same things to boys and that sometimes they say it together and get under the covers and play with each other. What I am saying is that just because this takes place doesn't mean *necessarily* that alarm bells need ring. The dangers lie in the business of coercion and bullying.

When my first son was about four, he used to play 'Doctors'

with the girl next door. She was the same age. The game seemed to involve, at some point, the pair of them getting into bed together and doing a 'medical' examination on each other. I'm not sure who invented the game but it was certainly something that interested both of them. The girl came round often and of her own accord. I couldn't see that there was any harm being done. In the girl's family, the little children often walked about naked and I remember on one occasion the smallest girl, who was only one at the time, sitting on the sofa with no nappy playing with herself, and her aunt, a victim of Down's Syndrome, sitting there giggling and laughing with the little girl. I will confess to being surprised at the time, but everyone seemed to think it was a big joke and, in hindsight, I can't see any harm in it. Certainly the air was free of shame, guilt and anxiety.

My last child, a boy, discovered his willy in public and used to sit on the sofa at bedtime playing with it. Sometimes it would stand up and my children being rather direct and comical started to cheer. For a while this became a kind of home party trick. The little chap would sit on the sofa, his willy would stand up and the

other children would burst into applause. Again, I can't see anything wrong in this.

None of this is to deny the problems of abuse. Any unwanted touching of another person is abuse and the moment that it happens, it damages. It crushes people's sense of identity and their sense of self-worth and can turn people to all kinds of chronic dependency and compulsive behaviour. I can easily understand that many parents might say, 'Surely it's safer to ban all physical sexual behaviour between children *in case* what is going on is abuse.' The problem is that if what is going on isn't abuse, but nothing more than a bit of shared curiosity and pleasure, then to prevent it altogether might be a damaging act too, suggesting that there is something wrong with our bodies and that sex is something naughty or bad.

My feeling, then, is that an absolute position like 'all touching is bad,' is not very useful. Some is and some isn't. As parents, it's our job to discriminate on all kinds of matters – clothes, food, TV programmes, sports – so why not on this matter too? Choices will have to be made in the light of who is involved, how old they are, how often it happens and how should we talk about it? This is, after all, a kind of sex education too.

Some people are worried about any or all of the following:

Is there a time when it is too young to start educating children?
I don't think so. Sex is the kind of knowledge that evolves. You start off with certain kinds of knowledge and then you add to it and change it as you get older. If, say, you tell a young child that making a baby needs a seed from the man and an egg from the woman then it's quite likely they will think the seed is like the seed of a flower and the egg is like a hen's egg. If you say the seed is like a tadpole then, if they have seen a tadpole, they will think that is what is inside dad's testicles. There is no absolute right and wrong way to tell the story, it starts out with ideas and shapes and will become altered as their bodies grow, they read books, they hear other versions, see 'rude' movies and so on.

Should you leave it entirely to the school?
I wouldn't. Not because the school version will be no good but because the school version will inevitably be less personal and

less to do with how each individual came to be made. The school version will try to be 'culture-free' by expressing it in medical terms, and, because of new government guidelines, to put sex in the sole context of family life. It may be that the medical terms seem strange and intimidating, whereas at home you can use family words which make it more real and warm. Also, what is the official version of 'family life' might not correspond to your set-up or how it was that your child was made, so you might need to modify some of the statements being made at school. Or even if your set-up is as is thought desirable by the guidelines, you might still want to explain that many people live and have sex in very different ways. With all the attention that sex crimes and sex in general has in the press and on TV, there are bound to be plenty of questions that children don't know the answers to, and school might not be able to provide.

Should I be worried about what teachers might say?
Once again this is partly a question of culture. Most teachers will be talking from a semi-medical point of view, where all body parts and processes can be given names and described. They may also say that it is desirable or usual that sexual intercourse goes on between a man and a woman who are committed to each other. You may not find this acceptable because you don't want your child to know such things until they are sexually mature. To which I would say, hard luck, because the children have already discussed it in the playground. Added to that, they may well have got certain vital parts of the story completely wrong. Social workers find that there are still thousands of teenagers who don't actually know what happens when males and females get together. However, once again, under the new guidelines, you are within your rights to withdraw your child from 'sex ed.'

On the other hand, you might find the restriction of sexual education to heterosexual married sex as misleading and too narrow because it doesn't actually describe what is going on out there. If so, then you can have a go at supplementing what the school offers as and when such things crop up in the news, or when a rumour goes round at school that, for example, 'kissing makes babies' or 'you can get AIDS from the dentist' and so on.

Siblings

There's a strange thing that people often say about families when siblings turn out with very different personalities – most sensationally expressed when relatives talk to the press about the trauma of having a sibling who is discovered to have murdered someone. 'Strange,' people say, 'you'd never have guessed they came from the same family.' But they don't. In one very important sense people 'of the same family' are not the same, because everyone's situation within a family is different. There is only one 'youngest child'; in a family of three children, there is only one 'middle child' and so on. Life can look very different if you're born first or last. The world is revealed to you in a very different way. It's why psychologists describe the experience of the older child having a new baby brother or sister as one of 'dethronement' or, in French popular culture, the youngest spoilt child is called 'le petit Benjamin', after Benjamin in the Bible.

I used to think that I was the younger brother in a family of four. I saw myself as the youngest in the house, two parents, two sons – perfect symmetry. Then one day, when I was about ten, my brother and I were going through old photos when we came across a picture of my mother with a baby on her lap. I said, 'Who's that? Brian [my brother] or me?' My father took a closer look at the photo and said, 'It isn't either of you. It's the baby who died.' It was the first time either my brother or I had heard about this. Our father explained that it was during the war and he went down with whooping cough. There were complications and they couldn't save him.

Looking back, there is a sense in which I became a different person at that moment. Though my parents and everyone else who had known them at that time, knew me to be the child my parents had after one that had died, I hadn't known that. There must have been all sorts of ways in which I (and of course my brother too) were treated that reflected this tragic situation. Some of the things that spring to mind: there was a time when my brother had pneumonia and he was kept in bed for what seemed like an age. I can see to this day the worry on my mother's face when the doctor came. Then again, there were ways in which I was a bit of a spoilt brat. My mother was always making allowances for me, explaining away occasions when I was a pain in the neck. It became a family joke, so that whenever my mother used to start giving excuses for some obnoxious thing I was doing, my father and brother would chant in a pseudo-sympathetic parody, 'Leave him alone, he's tired.' Or they would call me 'Little Mickie.' By the time I was six foot one and playing rugby this took on new levels of irony and absurdity.

Then again, like all younger brothers and sisters, I had a privileged view of what it was like to grow up as a child of my parents: I was my brother's spectator as he learnt the ropes. Every time he was told off, every time he approached some testing time or another – like, say, going to secondary school – I could watch and see how it turned out. I could consciously or unconsciously say to myself, 'I won't do it that way', or 'When I'm his age I'll have a go at that.'

This is all given another twist by the fact that, from the parents' point of view, siblings are treated differently. With first children we have all the anxiety and concern that comes with trying things out for the first time. Right from those first moments when we handle the newborn, there's every chance that it will be different from first to second child. By the time I came along, my parents had experienced the first, tentative try-out times with my brother, then came the feelings of loss and, perhaps, some awful sense of self-blame with the second, and then me. Never mind being spoilt – I must also have been an object of extra concern.

One aspect of being the youngest, in my case at any rate, was that I looked to my brother, four years older than me, as a kind of teacher. Some older children actively reject their younger brothers and sisters. Older siblings can spend the entire rest of their lives, after new siblings arrive, outraged that their parents could have been so wicked as to smash up the happy unit by bringing some-

one else in to the club. Maybe my brother had a double surprise – or perhaps trauma – of the initial 'dethronement', followed by the death of the new baby. When I came along it seemed to elicit in my brother a strong feeling of wanting to bring me on. Right from as early as I can remember my brother reckoned that whatever he knew, whatever he had learnt, it was his job to pass it on to me. When I was three he was teaching me how to read, when I was twelve he was trying to teach me calculus. But more than that, whatever he was going through, whatever ups and downs were going on in his life, he would tell me about in monologues, mimes and ravings. He was an addict of funny books and would read these out loud to me, adopting the different voices and acting out the parts. In many respects I was brought up as much by my brother as my parents. One downside of this was that he always appeared to me as an unbelievably skilled bloke. A younger child can easily get into a frame of mind that there isn't any point in attempting anything because older brother or sister is already doing it and much better. You think you'll never catch up. I didn't. I never got any good at making model cars and aeroplanes.

I find the hardest thing to do with my own children is to know how to intervene when they are arguing. As I've mentioned (*see*

ROWS), it's through arguing that they get to know who they are and what they think about the world. It's also through arguing that children hear from other people what kind of effect they are having on the world. If we work to the principle that we should stop them arguing at all times, then all this valuable stuff will be blocked off from them.

Then again, as our children get older the reasons for arguing change. There was a time when our two youngest were inseparable. The youngest looked up to his older sister and thought she was wonderful and brilliant and the most important person in the world. They played peacefully and creatively together all the time. But when the older one became a 'pre-teenager' then playing with a little boy who was mad about football, computers and *The Beano* started to seem a bit of a drag. Meanwhile, hair combing, Top of the Pops, the tightness of leggings and Doc Martens didn't seem all that terribly interesting to him. All sorts of squabbles would break out all over the place. While driving them to school they would have conversations that went like this:

HIM: Volvos are Swedish.

HER: I know that. It was me who told you that.

HIM: No it wasn't. I read it in a book.

HER: That was my book and I pointed it out to you in the book.

HIM: I know it's your book but I was reading it before you told me it was in there. I knew before that.

HER: No you didn't. You were surprised when I told you because you thought Volvos were American.

HIM: No I didn't. I knew they were Swedish.

HER: That's just lies.

These conversations are all about a change in the pattern of their companionship and his dependence on her. She wants to remind him that he is reliant on her for certain kinds of wisdom. He wants to say that he doesn't need it anymore. On other days she will say things to remind him of the opposite, that she doesn't want him to think that he is dependent on her anymore. Meanwhile, he thinks that he knows more than she gives him credit for.

All this can drive you completely barmy, listening to it going on in the back of the car on the way to school. But what would be gained by my telling them to shut up or that it doesn't matter? Not a lot. And obviously the conversation isn't really about Volvos.

Sleep-overs

From about the age of nine, I loved spending the night at friends' houses. Mostly this wasn't school friends but boys whose parents were friends of my parents. So this would involve exciting trips across London to the Finchley Road, Muswell Hill and North Harrow. In fact it was exciting for lots of reasons: the long bus journey, parental figures who wouldn't tell me off, different food, late nights giggling in the dark, the chance to tell each other all sorts of stories about kids we knew without any danger of it getting back to them. It was a way of growing up, a way of getting a perspective on family life that helped me weigh up different ways of behaving, different ways of eating, talking, dressing and getting told off. In toto, it helped me develop a sense of self.

So when our children ask to spend the night with friends I find myself overcome with nostalgia for those times: the treats that Malcolm's mother used to leave out at night on our bedside boxes, the joke that Chris's mother played on me with the plastic fried egg, the late-night farting contests, the discussions about teachers' and parents' lives, fantasies of revenge on bullies, romances with classroom beauties, sporting achievements.

That's the nostalgia. What about the reality now with children of my own? The questions I ask myself are: do I know the parents? Do I know whether the parents will be there any of the time, some of the time, all of the time? Children will happily conspire and plot moments of complete freedom which they might well use as an opportunity to wreck the joint. This happened to one of mine until I found out, too late. If you have reasonable reservations about the other family's set-up, or you aren't sure that the parents will be there all the time, then it's no big deal to say no, even if it causes tantrums. We are entitled to say no, but a child is entitled to know the reason why. Perhaps you aren't happy that you know the couple go to the pub on a Saturday night and the kids will be left alone in the house. We should say no and say why. Perhaps you feel threatened that your child's stay is going to give him or her a base from which to judge you. Say yes and shut up!

I insist on rules about phonecalls here. It's my experience that with the added confidence such visits give children, they start to get cocky and think that they don't have to tell you exactly where they are, or when they are coming back or why they are late. You have to stay firm on this one. No more sleep-overs unless you keep to the rules. Life's too dangerous otherwise. The other rule is that when they come bouncing back, it's my experience that they start being beastly to you, and to their younger brothers or sisters, the cat or the wall. Once again, the deal is: if sleeping-over turns you into a little sod, then no more sleep-overs.

'You never let me do what I want, you just make up any old rules you like. Hannah can do what she wants. Her parents don't stop her doing this, stop her doing that. What's the matter with you? Are you some kind of control freak? I hate you.'

'The answer to all those questions is yes, goodnight.'

I have found that the first urge my children have had to ask for sleep-overs occurs when they're about eight but I hear of others, especially when it involves cousins, where it has been at any time from about four. In one sense it doesn't really make much difference whether they are four or fourteen, you still have to feel right about it, you still have to be as near as certain that they won't be in any danger in the sleep-over house and that your lives won't be a misery the morning after.

Sport

We live in a country that is madly interested in sport but not in sport for everyone. We have hours of sport on the box, going out to watch live sport is still very popular, yet we do not have either the culture or public policy that encourages everyone to take part in some kind of active sport at least once a week. And by 'everyone' I mean infants, children, disabled, pensioners, parents, teenagers – everyone. So the word sport doesn't mean 'something we all do'. It means Manchester United, Olympic Games, World Championships, motor racing, horse jumping and Lords cricket ground. Of course there are millions of people who do play football in the local park, go swimming, jogging and the like but most of them are young men or people who are making a special effort about fitness.

All this sets up some very tricky problems for children. It means that collectively, through the media, school and home, we put on to children the idea that to take part in sport involves being either brilliant or a failure, and that to be beaten is to be unworthy. This means we have the splendidly ironic situation in which thousands of unfit old men sit around complaining about 'our' failure to win enough gold medals, the Football World Cup or a Test Match. The real failure is that millions of us, who may or may not be sad that national teams don't make the grade, don't keep fit enough to keep our blood flowing round our bodies, or strong enough to stop our backs killing us.

So when we talk about sport and children the question to ask of ourselves is, are we are giving them something to do which will simply make them feel worse than others – never quite good enough – or are we giving them something that they can enjoy doing for the rest of their lives? When there is talk of making team games compulsory for secondary-school children, it completely fails to get to grips with any of this. Millions of kids standing about on cold pitches never getting sight of the ball, being laughed at for having weedy legs, simply guarantees that millions of people leave school never to take part in sport ever again.

I say this as someone who as a child was what my brother called a KBU – keen but useless. I was desperate to be good at football but was slow, uncoordinated and clueless. I was quite good at swimming but there was no outlet for it but to go to the pool and play horrible tricks on younger children. Only as a teenager did I find some things to do that gave me any sense of self-worth in sport. As an adult I've taken part in sport in stops and starts. At the moment I'm in a stop. Most people I know are in a similar position or worse. So when we ask our children to take part in sport, what kind of model are we offering them? Are we asking them to perform for our benefit, to make up for our own lack of activity? How many fat, out-of-breath parents do we see on touchlines screaming at their children to get stuck in, make more effort, show a bit of spirit? Or, for that matter, lugging their children off to swimming lessons, ice-skating, gym class and the like but who wouldn't dream of diving in themselves? The message we give to children in such circumstances is that active sport is exclusively for kids. Apart from Linford Christie, adults are too busy or too serious to bother.

When we encourage children to take up sport we have to try and take all this on board. There is every likelihood that your child will come back from school at one time or another in a state of anxiety and/or anger about sport. He or she will feel unnecessarily cajoled, sneered at, or pushed too hard. At the same time, that same child, like all children, could well do with a bit of confidence-boosting, enjoyable, physical activity. How to resolve these contradictions?

PE at school may or may not be any good for our children. You have to be prepared for as much frustration as pleasure. Inner-city children like mine have terrible facilities for outdoor games: tiny playgrounds with no grass or the children have to make long journeys to astroturf pitches. Because of the pressure from government, TV sport and indeed many parents, there is great pressure to get in The Team but there aren't the time, space or resources to run enough teams for everyone. So producing The Team means elation for a few, frustration for many. (And indifference for plenty of others.) Some children are now leaving school not even knowing how to swim. The range of sport on offer to children is not as wide as it could be, especially in primary schools. The lack of money in primary education means that fewer and fewer men are teaching primary so less football is being played in primary schools. (This situation may change in the future with more women and girls becoming interested in playing football.) Primary schools are usually very good at offering fun team games like mat-ball, but not so good at offering the kinds of games that can be played in pairs like badminton and table tennis. This means that as children get older they don't necessarily know how to take part in a sport that just involves a friend or two.

So where does all this leave us? It's no use being over-ambitious. It's no use expecting more from kids than we expect of ourselves. If you're a sport freak, it may not be right to expect or demand of them as *much* as you do from yourself. If you like ball games and you play one regularly, then it's great to share it with your children, teaching them ball skills, and this of course enables them to take part in ball-games at school. But for goodness sake put the emphasis on skill and not on competition. If you go to watch your kid play, don't make their performance a matter of proving them worthy of your love or pride. I tend not to go and see them play simply in order to make up for the fact that I was rubbish myself.

As there is every chance that your child's school will not be able to provide a wide range of sports then you can try introducing some sports that are *not* on offer. We've tried not to do this at random, but looked at the child's body and temperament. Your child may have a great sense of balance but be no good at ball games. So ice-skating might be just right. You may think your child is overweight. Swimming might be good. I was a fatty, and very slow on land, but could get through the water efficiently enough. Sports centres have badminton days and it's a good game for mixed ages, boys and girls playing together. Judo and karate, when taught well in clubs, can transform unconfident children.

Whatever you opt for, you are likely to come up against the problem of competition. The better your child gets at a sport, the greater the pressure from school, club or you for him or her to join a team and compete against others. Your child may not want to be competitive. She may just have wanted to get good. This has happened to several of my children who enjoyed getting good at football, swimming and ice-skating. The moment the adults around them spotted this, they started trying to corral them into teams, get them to train harder, become more competitive and the like. It turned them right off and they quickly got into poolside sulking and being unable to get up for Saturday morning footy training. I'll admit to being frustrated. There was one part of me that wanted them to have a go, get stuck in, push themselves. But there was another part of me that said, hang on, there is really no point in getting into all that competitive stuff unless your heart is really in it. Being an avid competitor doesn't make you a better person or better able to cope with life. It really is a bit ripe having to listen to alcoholic retired footballers and cricketers, with strings of wrecked personal lives behind them, telling us that team sports build character and make you better able to cope with life.

Then there's the problem of a child who *does* want to be competitive, does want to join a team but no matter what you do to support them they just aren't good enough. This often happens to boys who are desperate to get good at football. For many boys this is not just so that they can get into the team but so that they can be accepted as 'real' boys. Being good at football is a test of one's masculinity. It's tough to bear if you're no good. As a parent, you may well end up taking your boy to football practice not because he's good but so as to make him less bad, in the hope that he will feel less of a nerd, be less likely to be left out, not picked on in the playground knock-arounds. We've had a few tears on this particular path.

With pre-teenage girls it can be a struggle getting them interested in using their bodies for something other than staring at in the mirror. Anyone who has ever had anything to do with sport will tell you that most pubescent girls in our culture do their best to avoid most forms of physical activity apart from dancing. Run with it. If they don't want to play football, badminton, tennis, do gym or anything like that then suggest ice-skating, roller-skating, or any kind of dance that doesn't seem fuddy-duddy or out of date. There's a sexist agenda here too. One of the reasons many girls opt out of physical activity is that unconsciously they are making themselves less threatening to boys, more 'feminine', more vulnerable, weaker, and generally occupying less space. To be fragile, weak and eyelid-fluttering is still seen as the way to get the guy. It's also the way to be dominated and less self-reliant. We know that girls as young as ten are going under with eating disorders: anorexia, bulimia and obesity. Sport isn't a solution – 'make her play football, that'll shake her out of it' – but finding some kind of physical activity that gives the girl a sense of enjoyment out of using her body and encourages a sense of self-worth might help.

Starting Nursery

If you're lucky you live in an area where children have nursery places available from any time between the age of three and school admission at 'rising five'. For something like a hundred years there have been occasional political flurries about how desirable this would be for all children. It has been said many times that two years extra at the youngest end of schooling would help more children to be confident about reading and writing. With this in mind, if you can't get your children into a state nursery class or school, and if you're someone who spends money on a nanny or minder, then you might look at the cost of having your child in a private nursery for a few hours a week. If you haven't got either a nanny or the money then you will, quite rightly, wonder why it is that Britain, unlike many other countries, hasn't got the political will to improve things. Perhaps it's part of a general culture that regards small children as less important than bigger ones, and they in turn less important than university students and all of them less important than adults.

So, you're one of the lucky ones and you arrive for your first day at a nursery. To my knowledge the time has long since passed when you were expected to dump your child and run. Most nurseries that I know have been quite happy for first parents to stay as long as they want with their child, both in the sense of as long as they want on a single day, and for as long as they want over a period of a few weeks. No doubt if you become over-protective or objectionable then nursery teachers and assistants are trained to ask you to leave but mostly, in my experience, it's been a lovely time. I've enjoyed sitting on the floor, making phonecalls

in the Home Corner, pushing swings, doing sticky-fingers paint work and the like.

It may seem like an extravagant use of time, that you really are too busy to do this sort of thing, but as with so much of what happens with children, it is a tiny proportion of your and their lives. Being a freelance, it was much easier for me to stay at the nursery than many other parents, but if it is possible for you to be more 'flexi' with your time then this is a period well worth making space for. Not only do you help your child settle. You get to see him or her in relation to a wider circle than just friends and family, you meet other parents, and you learn how your child copes with all these new faces and experiences.

I have sat in with four of my children during their early days at nursery. For each of them it was a short time but full of significance. How small they were but how full of thoughts and concerns. I'm glad I was there.

I should add here that there is a special importance about your coming and going from nursery. Even if your child is used to saying goodbye to you when you leave them with a childminder, nursery schools are very different places. There will be so many more people and so much more going on. How you greet the teacher, how the teacher greets you and your child, how you say goodbye to your child and how you greet your child when you come back at the end of nursery, are all highly significant. The child will want to see in your face and body language that you trust the teacher and like her. He or she will probably, at first, want a good cuddle and kiss, not the old peck-and-run treatment that I've seen some people delivering. Children on the receiving end of that sometimes express their anxieties later in the class by being withdrawn or niggly. When you turn up to collect your child, it's important to give him or her full eye contact either by getting down on their level or lifting them up to yours. It means, I'm glad to see you. I want to see you. Have you got anything to say? I've got something to say to you. Comings and goings are very important.

Starting School

I don't know what it is about my legs but nearly all my children have found that on their first day at school they are very useful. They're not too big for two small arms to completely encircle and yet not too small to seem too feeble to be worth hanging on to. The scene usually runs: child comes into school holding hand, into the classroom gripping hand, sits down hugging leg. I've noticed that this makes some mums and dads embarrassed – I don't mean they're embarrassed by my leg but by theirs. It's because we've got this puritan, stiff-upper-lipped thing whereby the first day at school becomes a kind of exhibition for thrusting, self-reliant children. If my child sobs and screams it proves that he's a little weed and I've failed to bring him up prepared to win contracts and climb Mount Everest. You can't escape it. All the parents are glancing across the room checking how hard other children are hugging their parents' legs, how many tears their one has shed compared with yours. And when the teacher says, 'Right, this is the book corner,' you're desperate for your kid to quietly stand up, walk across to the books and say, 'Ah, *The Jolly Postman*, just what I've been looking for.' And you will feel like an inadequate parent if she stares at the book corner like it's a Rottweiler kennel and then hides her head in your lap.

The truth of the matter is that it isn't your kid who's in a state, it's YOU. How dare she grow up? She might turn into someone who can go somewhere where it's not you she'll be asking when she wants a Kleenex. And what if she gets really fond of the nursery teacher and you start having conversations that go like this:

YOU: Looks a bit cloudy today, I expect it'll rain later.

YOUR CHILD: My teacher says that it won't rain today.

or:

YOU: One and one makes two.

YOUR CHILD: My teacher says one and one makes five.

YOU: Er, I don't think she said that.

YOUR CHILD: She did.

YOU: Look here, I've been around on this planet for nearly forty years and though your nursery teacher is one of the most brilliant, loving and beautiful people ever to have lived, I'm telling you that one and one makes two. And what's more, I am telling you here and now that your brilliant, loving and beautiful teacher – who I should add has been on this planet one or two years less then me – would agree one hundred per cent with me on this matter.

YOUR CHILD: Wouldn't.

For many of us who have brought our children up in the small nuclear family set-up, the first day at school is both an actual and a symbolic break. For people who are used to sharing their children with grannies, grandads, nannies, aunties, uncles and friends, it's less of a wrench, less of a relinquishing of control. But either way, school is different from home, childminders and even playgroup. Over the last few years, it's my experience that the first few months of 'real' school – now called Year 1 – have become much more schooly. Much less time is spent on painting, acting, clay-work, singing, dance or any of the creative activities and much more time is spent sitting down, sitting still and practising letters and numbers. Some people will think this is a good thing and a great advance and will guarantee that their child will become Einstein. Whether it's good or bad in the long run, it means that the first days in Year 1 now require you to deal with the very real possibility that your child will sometimes come home tense, bored, frustrated and lacking in self-confidence. Education of young children has become much more task-oriented and teachers are more worried that parents will be breathing down their necks if their five-year-old can't read encyclopaedias and do algebra: 'Hey look here, when I was four I was reading Homer in the original Greek. What are you doing about that, eh?' All this feeds into First Day Fever too: teachers are worried that you're worried. You're worried that the teacher is too worried. Your child is worried that you're worried that the teacher's worried.

I exaggerate.

Whatever it's really like, what can you do to ease the passage? The first thing to remember is that from a child's point of view the worry is less about hard sums or long books than about *relationships*. Will the teacher be nice? Will the children in my class be nice? So the ideal preparation is, if possible to get to know some of the other children going to that school and that class. And – harder – get into the school for your child to meet the teacher before the First Day. This is much more important than trying to do some pre-school home teaching so that when the teacher says: 'Spell the word "diocese"' your child will know the answer. Pre-school home tuition, trying to fit into an imagined curriculum, will only create anxiety for you and your child. Forget it.

This is not to say do nothing on the learning front. Once again, ideally, we should work on the principles of creativity, pleasure and imagination. This means offering children a variety of activities: board games, painting, scribbling (yes), books, comics, plasticene, play dough, cooking, going out to see story tellers, puppet shows, theatre shows, playing ball games, climbing games, going to museums, nature trails, open farms. Any child who has done all these kinds of things between the ages of three and five (ideally with one or two friends of his or her own age) will be much better prepared for that First Day than the one who has been made to fill in those spelling and maths books you see on sale everywhere now.

I suppose I wanted my children to start school in a state of mind where they could make friends, not be frightened by teachers, not be bowled over if a teacher asked them to do something and have enough belief in themselves not to panic or get miserable if things got tough. I wanted that, but it didn't happen. One of them always regarded a teacher asking her to do something as a kind of death sentence. For a few years she became very good at responding to teachers with a kind of toxic-shock look. When asked 'What's up love?' she would go limp.

My oldest – now eighteen – said that going to school was a great surprise to him. For the first few years of his life, he told me, he had a really great time. He went to the zoo, went to shows, had a good laugh. Then school happened to him and, he said, 'It wasn't funny. School just wasn't a funny place.'

'Hang on a minute,' I said. 'Do you mean school wasn't *fun?*'

'No,' he replied, 'I mean school wasn't *funny*.'

'Look,' I said, 'school isn't supposed to be funny. It's not a comedy show, you know.'

'Yes, yes,' he said. 'I know that now, but the whole time I was at school I was always wanting to have a good laugh and it never happened.'

Oh no, I thought, that was my fault. Maybe in the first five years of his life I lulled him into thinking that life is a laugh, that every day you're entitled to four good giggles and at least one belly laugh. Clearly, the passage of home to school is not often smooth.

Back to that First Day itself. Some schools allow parents into the classroom and, within reason, to hang about, settling your child down and leaving only when it feels OK to do so. Others

treat you like an enemy spy who must be repelled at all costs: throw your child over the wall at nine o'clock and we will throw him or her back at half past three. If you're allowed in, try to find a book and sit with your child for a while looking at the pictures and talking about it. When I leave, I try to be clear that I'm going now – yes, now. I will think of you all day and I (or whoever is doing the picking up) will be there at going-home time. If they trust us in other things in life then it's unlikely that they will start distrusting us now. If on the other hand you are muddled or shifty about going, you dither, or you forget to say who is coming to pick them up, then you make it tough for the child. If your child is wildly clinging and does completely break up, then one or two days of this happening is no big deal. But if it goes on, then they may rightly or wrongly be untrusting of you. You may have to think what might have happened that they should doubt your word.

One of my children started his first day in Year 1 not very long after I had separated from my first wife. I'm not going to boast that it was all hunky-dory or that he didn't worry when I left him at school but I am prepared to flatter myself this far: by being aware that his main anxiety would be that one or both of his parents were about to disappear over the horizon and desert him, I and my ex both worked hard to reassure him of the opposite, that one or other of us would always be there for him. This often meant (for me) sitting up with him till nine or ten o'clock at night because he didn't want to see me go out of the bedroom door and . . . perhaps never come back? A First Day at school while this is going on needs a lot of reassurance.

Step-brothers and -sisters

This is a growth industry. The five children who have lived with me are variously step-brothers, step-sisters, half-brothers and half-sisters. Many a happy teatime has been spent discussing who is to what and what is to whom. They've invented people called half-cousins and step-uncles. In the past, these kinds of relationships were dark secrets. I know a man of my generation who was told that someone was his step-brother but he found out later he was his son. Work that one out if you can! There are people who were told that new arrivals in the house were real sisters who in fact turned out to be half-sisters and the whole business was surrounded with shame. One can only hope that as a first principle we can eliminate shame from the business. I sometimes detect a little embarrassment around the fringes of our family when strangers start asking who is the daughter of whom. As people stumble and bumble through apologies and 'No, no. No offence meant . . .' we end up having to relieve people of *their* blushes at the very moment when they think they are relieving ours. I mean it's no big deal is it?

People have different sexual partners through their lives and sometimes this leads to children. In general, these parents then set about working out ways to bring these children up. So first, please, no shame. And that means no shame in front of children. That, in turn, means openness about where children came from biologically. My wife adopted a wonderful scheme to make this openness clear and public: the Life Book. All the children have Life Books that start from birth, with photos – and it could be mementoes and scraps as well. The children can see their lives, and all the people who have had something to do with them, in full Kodacolour – deserting fathers, wayward uncles, dubious friends who mysteriously disappeared when they disapproved of something or other – all can be found, talked about and laughed over. Dates of appearances and disappearances explain just who was with whom and when and so fantasies about, say, how recent or how long ago events occurred can be ironed out. These Life Books provide a bedrock of reality in what can easily lapse into a fog of fantasy, anxiety, and plain lies.

So there you are, face to face with step-children. It's now the regular subject matter of children's fiction and TV drama. Here the plot usually runs by beginning with enmity and ending with compromise. In one extraordinary teenage version, it ends in sex between the steps. In one current TV drama, it is straight war. In my gang, the main problems are between the half-siblings not between the steps. There are many more rows between the kids who share a mother but not a father than there are between the kids who don't share any 'real' parents. It seems as if between the steps there is still just a tiny bit of courtesy left, a tiny bit of distance that makes allowances. Between the half-siblings there is heaps of unfinished business like: how dare you be born? You didn't ask my permission. And in reply: why do you try to boss me about, I'm not your servant. Don't keep nicking my things, you don't own me or my things.

Some steps take all their resentment of the way in which their parents have split up and taken up with other partners *without consulting them* and channel it into hate of the new step-siblings. The girls say that younger step-brothers are nerds and creeps. Older boys say younger step-sisters are spoilt brats who fancy themselves. Step-brothers say of each other that they're freaks, dweebs, snobs, slimeballs. Step-sisters say of each other that they love themselves, they're stuck up, they're swots and so on . . . It can be tense. It has to be said that these dislikes – even hatreds – may in many instances never get better, never end peaceably and on some occasions get worse as they grow into adulthood when there is dark talk of inheritances and unfairness.

Some people say that you have to say to steps who don't get on to just buck up, accept reality or shut up. Most of the hatred, they say, is displaced anger about the split-up and the new liaison. If you allow yourself to give in to the resentments, then you feed the child's fantasies about you getting back with your estranged partner, or at the very least, splitting up with the present one. You mustn't give in to this egocentric blackmail, the line goes, or you'll never be able to live your own life. Ten or fifteen years later, when the child has grown up, you'll regret it like crazy as you sit all alone thinking about the super lover you lost because he or she got fed up with your kid being horrible to his or her kid. And anyway your kid doesn't love you any the more for having given in to his or her demands. In fact he or she thinks you're a bit of a prat.

It's quite a powerful argument but of course you can't make it a hard and fast rule. Maybe life really has become intolerable for your child. Not only because you've broken up all his certainties. It may be that his new step-sibling *is* an intolerable little creep who is up to all sorts of sneaky little tricks and your own child is being driven completely crazy by the way that neither you nor the new step-parent ever does any telling-off. What do you do? Ignore what's going on? Offer a few 'cheer-up darlings' and have another drink?

It may be tiring and time consuming but situations like these really do call for family meetings. Half-hours, hours, days even, where everyone sits round and talks. Everyone has to listen, everyone has the right to speak no matter how old or young. It may not solve everything. It may solve very little. But you can be sure of one thing: little cabals, furtive alliances between him and her against her and her, secret tête-à-têtes in the bathroom will all make matters worse. There have been times when we've had to have family councils to solve matters like whether one of the children was allowed into another child's room when that child was away at his or her other parent's place. It was a vital matter concerning privacy and a sense of home. To the child who did the invading, it seemed perfectly okay to pile in there and grab stuff if the usual occupant wasn't there and wasn't using it. To the child whose room it was it seemed like a horrible arrogance, and it wrecked any fragile sense that this new place was home. It was a perfect example of the way an alliance, usually between the biological parent and the biological child, can make matters worse. It needed a whole-family resolution and agreement of the problem.

Do step-parents have the same rights over step-children as

they do over their biological children? Probably not. It's much better to be honest with step-children. Don't pretend to be as good or as nice as the 'real' mother or father who may have fled, may be living down the road or may have died. He or she may be the biggest shit in the world but you nonetheless shouldn't pretend to be the 'real' one. Establish some other way of going on. There are certain decisions concerning my step-daughters that I withdraw from: final steps that in the end have to be resolved between the girls and their mother. These might be about choice of school, clothes, subjects taken at school, what clubs and societies to join. This is not to say I am completely indifferent or mute. I am quite prepared to join in discussions, throw in my tuppenny-worth, but at the end of the day I'm not the one who shakes on the final agreement. No matter how absent the real father is, I am not pretending to be more than a step-parent. It frees up me and them to relate more clearly. Sometimes we want to be affectionate with each other, sometimes angry, and both sides know that it doesn't and won't affect the really big decisions which are made in tandem with their mother. And it means it doesn't invade whatever feelings and fantasies they have about their father. Maybe I'm deluding myself here. One day, when they're much older, they'll say what they think about this semi-detached way of going on; but at the moment it feels right to me.

It also puts down markers for my own biological children. In their own ways, they both showed unhappiness and resentment when I split up with their mother and got together with my present wife. They felt usurped by their step-sisters who seemed to be getting a bigger slice of me than they got. Quite often they didn't tell me this but said things to their mother who then reported them back to me. They found holidays particularly galling. The system that my ex and I worked was half-and-half care, so we thought if they had a holiday with each of us in turn it would be fine. But I learnt that they would sometimes feel rotten about the holiday they weren't having with me while they were having one with their mother. And when they were with me on holiday they would, quite naturally, want to have plenty of long phonecalls to their mother. All we could do was make sure that we were open and consistent and that they had really good times on their holidays.

Returning to the matter of relationships with your 'biologicals' that are different from your steps, this sometimes leads to outbursts of resentment. From my wife I've had, 'Oh yes, we all know that everything your son does is perfect. He never does anything wrong.' If I'm absolutely honest (unpleasant thing to do) she has probably been right. Because I see them half the time, I sometimes think why waste it by being heavy? To the steps this looks like preferential treatment. There's also a little bother around the fact that children who aren't absolutely certain that you are a permanent, loving fixture will find it tougher to take blame and disapproval than children who are safe in the knowledge that you are forever. I remember one occasion when I had a row with my step-daughter about interrupting. It was, significantly, while I was having a conversation with one of my boys. I got ratty and sent her out and the next thing she was really angry and in tears. Her reaction was disproportionate to the row over the interruption and much more to do with being fed up about preferential treatment and not feeling one hundred per cent safe in her relationship with me.

What do you do about this? Pretence is yukky. You can't go about the house pretending that you love everyone equally if you don't. If you do, great, but if you don't it's ghastly. So all you can do is go for fairness in the rows and arguments, equality in matters of money, and openness about the fact that relationships *are* different and there are reasons from the past that explain that. After all, you can say, if you remember when I first turned up you though I was revolting and wouldn't speak to me. Or: when I first turned up you thought I was God and now you know I'm not.

My experience is in the area of what Americans call (would you believe?) the 'blended family'. Two of mine, two of hers and one of ours. But plenty of people have the job of coping with situations like 'three of his and none of mine' or 'one of mine and none of hers'. People say it's tough sometimes to fancy an adult and find that you have to take the whole package – him and the kid, her and the kids – or whatever. I guess it's tough because we are encouraged by romantic films and the like to see each other as coming into relationships with no strings, without parents, grandparents, ex-lovers, bosom friends and children. Part of the reason why we find films so appealing is that they shear off all that stuff called reality, all the messy stuff to do with trying to make a living and having a past and present linked inseparably to people other than the sexy newcomer. In my twenties I had a relationship with a woman with whom I was convinced I could have a really brilliant time if only she didn't have any relationships apart from the one with me. Very realistic! It's always an illusion, whether people have kids or not, that they can come into your life shedding all this. Kids get a worse press because they are physically in evidence, make demands and start expressing views about you. But what about the moment when you dare to express a view about how your partner is bringing up his or her kids? Dangerous territory! 'Who do you think you are coming in here and telling me how to bring up my children? I've been doing it my way, unaided, for the last three years. Just because you've moved in doesn't mean you can tell me where I'm going wrong. You've never even reared a pet mouse, let along three children . . .'

All very true BUT . . . Once you've moved in then the rules do change. Everyone does start commenting on how people treat each other. It's almost impossible to have a judgement-free relationship. We don't and can't live by simply saying, 'You do things your way, I'll do them my way.' That's called a not-relationship. But boy, living with someone who you feel is judging you and criticizing you without taking any judging themselves is a pain in the neck. And the biggest pain in the neck happens when people start judging each other about how they bring up their children. When things get really smelly and you're saying to her that she spoils her kids and she's saying to you that you're a cold fish or you're saying to him that he is his kids' poodle and he's saying to you that you're an insensitive jerk then it's probably time for a stand-off period. Though it might be impossible to conduct whole relationships on the basis of non-judgemental talk, it *is* possible to have breaks in the sparring and even rule some areas out-of-bounds. Deals can be struck: I won't have a go at you for this, if you don't have a go at me for that. Let's try that for a month. . . .

Step-children sometimes need help at school. All kinds of niggly bits of rubbish float around about whether 'that man who picks you up is your real father' and the like. You sometimes find that your kid has been lying about step-parents. Sometimes we

forget to give children words to describe people in their lives. Are you 'my dad's girlfriend'? 'my mum's partner'? 'Dave'? All the other kids are sitting there talking about 'Mum' and 'Dad' and you've got the problem of finding a snappy title for the newcomer, the appendage, the one you're not really very sure about anyway. We need to help here, not to leave children high and dry without some means of talking about the step-parent. It may be that even before the step-parent has got his or her feet fully under the table that we should still give our kids a handle. If you're clear about this, it makes it easier for the children to be clear about it in school and this in turn makes it less likely (but not impossible) that the other children will make it an issue. Even the slightest breath of nastiness should be talked about with your children's teacher. Firstly, your child, no matter what her relationships at home, is entitled to be accepted on an equal basis and, secondly, the other children, no matter what their home relationships, can learn from the different ways in which people are living. Teachers may be embarrassed about it and so you have to be quite clear with them that there is nothing to be embarrassed about. This is the way the world is and always has been. People live in many different ways and this is the way we are living now. The person who comes to pick up my children on Thursdays is their 'step-father' or 'my partner' or whoever. You can always be sure of one thing: fibs, fudging, secrets and shame are far, far more corrosive than openness. If there is one kid who is particularly persistent, then confront the kid, and/or the parent(s). It needs to be dealt with as soon as possible or your own children's lives will be made a misery and they'll come to hate school.

The children will also need terms for their step- and half-brothers and sisters. We shouldn't make them pretend that they are 'real' brothers and sisters when other children will keep telling them that they're not. What my kids have discovered is that if they are clear and open about the relationship from the beginning, the other children soon forget to make it an issue and call them brothers and sisters anyway. I have had children come running up to me at the school gate saying: 'You're not her real dad, are you?'

'No, I'm her step-dad.'

'So why does she call you Dad?'

'She knows I'm her step-father, you know I'm her step-father, but she can call me what she likes so long as it's not Fatbum.'

Teaching in school

I've spent fourteen years worrying about what my kids are doing in school. My first child decided at the age of six that school wasn't really a very good idea and spent the next ten years looking out of the window. I longed for there to be teachers who would engage his interest in maths problems, science experiments, stories, poems, social history or whatever. But no matter whether the teacher was brilliant or a freeloading jerk – no one ever caught his imagination. He says it's because he got fed up when he found out that 'school wasn't funny'. I think it's also when he found out that at school you can't do what you want to do. You can't find out the things you want to find out, you can't play the way you want to, you can't sit with the friends you want. He became a hippy at six and there wasn't much anyone could do about it.

I know this now but at the time it was worrying and sad. I could sense a tension in him between the kid that didn't want to disappoint his parents and the kid that wanted to daydream and play and explore things in his own way. Sometimes there were teachers who could see he was like that, and if they put pressure on him it only made things worse. When I look back at what he got from school, I am confused. No doubt there are some alternative private schools that would have suited his personality better but that would have encouraged in him the belief that it was Dad's job to subsidize him to be a daydreamer. No thanks. If he wants to be a daydreamer then he can earn the right to that all by himself.

At one point in his schooling I was in despair. His primary school was falling apart. A young and very capable classroom teacher had become headteacher and for reasons I can't figure out, she was a complete dead loss in this role. She couldn't keep staff at the school, she couldn't give new staff guidelines. The school books were disappearing out of the school at a rate of £2000 a year. Various unqualified nerds came in and tried anything from a mishmash of prep-school rote learning to 'please yourself kids, I'm going on a world trip soon.' The parents grew more and more restive. The board of governors proposed a vote of no confidence in the head. Meanwhile most of the teachers closed ranks to support the head and things got very nasty. In the end over thirty parents took their children away from the school and the head was moved sideways into research. Nearly ten years later there are ex-teachers from the school who look the other way when I see them in the streets.

Whenever I think back to that time I try to think whether we did the right thing, or whether things could have been done differently. When things started getting bad, and teachers were losing our kids' work, projects were getting torn up and put in the bin, music clubs were falling apart, projects weren't being finished, whole terms went by with no writing being done, the school library disappeared, I started writing letters. They were long, repetitive, hectoring, patronizing, arrogant and boring. I've no doubt, now, that they were the wrong thing to have done. The headteacher showed them to the other teachers, who were offended and rallied round the head and the classroom teacher whom I was criticizing.

As the weeks went by we gathered that most other parents were in a panic about what was going on. What took place then was much better. Parents put pressure on the parent governors who raised whatever they could in governors' meetings. Whenever it got too near the bone, however, these parent governors would be ruled out of order. So in the end these governors called a meeting of all the parents to discuss what should be done. Over a hundred parents attended. In the end a vote of no confidence wasn't passed but an ultimatum was put to the local education authority. In fact most of the parents didn't wait and got their children out that summer.

I reckon that my oldest – the daydreamer – lost two years of schooling at that school. Sometimes his mother and I blame ourselves for letting it go on so long but we were reluctant to pull him out because he had already changed schools once as a result of moving house. Sometimes we wonder if his experience there was so chaotic and discouraging that it knocked out of him the will to produce good pieces of work for the rest of his school career. We're not sure because he was already heading for Never-Never Land before he got to that school. In the end you never can be sure how much is your kid and how much is the school.

This was all before the days of the National Curriculum and SATs (Standard Assessment Tasks). The theory behind these is that they will eliminate schools like the one I've described. I don't see how. What that school needed was a lot of help. It needed the local authority or the inspectorate to move in with plans of action, classroom support, training sessions, parents' meetings and learning contracts. It needed some experienced teachers to come in and give talks and model lessons. The present system of league tables, threats of closure, lightning visits by inspectors, means demoralization and disruption. It doesn't make poor teachers better, nor does it use the talents of the experienced to help the inexperienced.

Today, with the primary school my children are at, and others that I visit, the main problem isn't incompetence – though no doubt there are some heads bumbling through in the way that my son's headteacher did. Parents and teachers alike know that the main problem is to do with lack of money and increasing class size. In my children's school, for instance, there is only one computer per class, and no CD-ROMs.

Of course your situation may be different in that you are also faced with incompetence on the part of the teaching staff. What do you do? Try and change what's going on or move your child out? Perhaps both. If you go for changing, don't try and do it on your own. Talk to other parents at the school, talk to parents at other equivalent schools and see if they are getting a better deal. See if you can sort out whether the problem is with your child's classroom teacher or with the head. If it is the classroom teacher, what do the other parents think? Have an informal meeting round at your house. If you're on your own then you'd better think about moving your child out. If you're all agreed, then raise the matter with your parent governors and/or the head. When

you raise the matter, bring up specific practical points, give actual examples of work, don't rely totally on hearsay from your child. Use comparisons with other classes, with other schools if need be. If a group of you have a meeting with the head, come to the meeting with examples of the children's work – or lack of it – so that you can argue about specific cases. Otherwise the dispute will disappear into waffle. Come with statistics about the lack of school visits to museums and places of interest, the lack of swimming and sport. Don't put yourselves in a position where you're saying: 'They don't seem to be doing any . . . these days' or you'll be steamrollered with denials.

If the issue seems to be headteacher incompetence, then only a large meeting with a majority of the parents and some of the teachers' tacit cooperation can get anything done. It will take an enormous amount of energy, determination and organization. You will lose friends and make enemies over it and no one will thank you for it. It might be simpler just to move schools.

Your best way of doing this is through gossip. You can visit a school as often as you like but you won't get the real feel of it until you talk to parents and children who go there. That said, on a visit you ought to be able to get a sense of how active the school is, what its priorities are and what its educational policy is on class-room organization, attitudes to children, and what kind of work they expect children to do.

When you go into a classroom, look at how busy the children are. Look at how much work seems to have been put up on the walls since the beginning of term. Look and see whether the teacher has resourced the room well for whatever is the project in hand. Have the children done any writing other than factual writing? Have they made books of their own? They should have done. Has the class been for any visits to museums or places of interest? They should have done.

How are the classes in the school organized? You should be able to get a feel for whether the classroom organization is help-ing the children to work quietly and in long stretches of concentration. It should also be enabling children to do work that they organize themselves and which doesn't simply come direct-ed from the teacher.

Are there facilities in the school that support extra-curricular learning and discovery – a garden? after-school sport? pets? on-site development of playgrounds, wall painting etc? How much emphasis does the school put on children's opportunities to play music, do drama, paint, write stories and poems, make news-papers, dance? Any or all of these activities are vital outlets of expression for your children that the curriculum may not supply.

Does the school have visiting singers, musicians, story-tellers, drama groups, children's writers? Does it organize special 'weeks' – book weeks, maths weeks and the like – where the cur-riculum is suspended and the children and parents can concen-trate on one area? Does the school have a bookshop? a parents' association? Does the school have a policy on inviting parents in to support school outings, concerts, fêtes etc? More importantly, does the school have a policy on learning partnerships between school and home? Are parents notified at the beginning of term what is going to be studied? Is parents' help called for?

What kind of evidence is there that the school is interested in science and technology? Have the children carried out any experiments? Have they designed anything? Have they been asked to invent something, or come up with solutions for local environmental problems like the local park or the polluted river? How many computers are there at the school and how are they used? Who gets a turn on them?

Does the school have a policy on equal opportunities? How does the school reflect the cultures of the children in it, in the local community, in Britain as a whole? If it has a multicultural intake, would it be possible to deduce this if you came into the school when there were no children there?

How is the discipline in the school? How are parents involved in that? How soon are they brought in when there is a problem?

All these are questions that you can ask or you can ask yourself as you walk round a school. Listen out for the way teachers talk to children. Are they yelling at children or does it look as if there's a policy of trying to run the school without shouting. Do children run about the school bumping into each other? Or do they walk about the place in a quiet sort of way?

I offer these questions as a way of sorting out what you want from a school. In an ideal world, I would like schools to be safe places where everyone treated each other with respect and children could find out how to learn. Other people have different priorities such as children should respect the teachers but it is not so important that the teachers respect the children, or that all children should learn how to respect all other children, no matter what their background. Some people think that it is less important that children find out how to learn than if children just learn things full stop. Some people are not worried sick by the unsafeness of schools because they were never very safe places in the past either. I hope that the questions above will serve as a focus no matter what your priorities.

See CHOOSING A SECONDARY SCHOOL for the separate problems here.

Their rooms

I once sat looking out of the window of an Australian house in the city of Perth thinking about rooms. We were in a suburb called Wembley which was divided up into quarter-acre blocks in the 1930s on which people built white concrete houses with curvy steps and fluted door frames. For a while I had a job at a college there. At the time the baby was in bed with us, the two girls shared a room and the two boys shared a room. I looked out of the window on to a lawn of what they call buffalo grass, a lemon tree, a white asbestos garage, the back entrance to a Chinese takeaway and liquormart and, I thought, when my brother reached twelve, we each got separate rooms. That was thirty years ago. I am better off than my parents were, my oldest son is nearly twelve and he can't have a room of his own. What am I doing wrong?

After this revelation, it became a kind of mantra: the boys must have rooms of their own. I had a room of my own, the boys must have rooms of their own. I think it bothered me much more than it bothered them. They went on sharing at their mother's house until the oldest one reached eighteen. I don't know whether there is a real watershed at twelve when children must have rooms of their own and that until then it's brilliant being in together. My feelings about this are all wrapped up with my own childhood, the garden in Wembley and the effort we put in to convert the house to give them a bedroom each. Rationality – forget it.

Sharing my bedroom with my brother seems to me now to be one of the most long-lasting and affecting things that has ever happened to me. My brother made our room into a theatre, model railway and model aeroplane exhibition space, a beer labels collection display and a sounding board for all matters of the heart. It was a dormer room under the eaves and my brother used its sloping surfaces to stick up posters and beer mats and beer labels that he steamed off bottles from the off-licence next door. In that room we invented massively crucial games like Who Had the Last Hit? and Last One Into Bed Has to Switch Out the Light. We rehearsed grotesque performances of Walter de la Mare's '"Is there anybody there?" said the Traveller, knocking on the moonlit door.' My brother read out passages and whole chapters from his favourite books like *Down with Skool* until we knew them off by heart. He would run through his complaints about teachers, bullies and our parents until I knew a whole cast of characters whom I had never met.

He did have the more comfortable bed. I don't know why that was. His bed was low-slung, modern and luxurious. When he got into it, he could snuggle down in it so that only his left eye peeked out; it always seemed warmer and safer in his bed. He told me how to make a bed warm without using a hot water bottle: you duck under the covers, bring your knees up as high as you can, breathe into the space between your head and your knees until it's hot, you release this hot bubble into the rest of the bed and start again. Do this about ten times and the bed's warm. But my bed was never as nice as his. I called my bed a 'potato bed'. It was higher off the floor and creaked.

There's a line in a Pinter play where one of the menacing characters stands over one of the feeble ones and says: 'You know what you are? A slug. A slum slug.' I can't think of the number of times when I've stood in the middle of my children's rooms and felt like saying it too. There's something blissfully unaware about the way children will quite happily let piles of Lego, dirty pants, Game Boys, football programmes, polythene bags, socks and more build up. They can quite happily get out of bed and step straight on to Lego models that took them hours to make. Treasured stones collected from a beach on holiday can be found in their beds. They watch beloved posters peel off the wall and hang, one corner down, Blue Tack blob showing, for weeks. When you say, 'Time for a clean-up in here,' they look hurt and mystified. 'What *is* there to clean up?' they think.

I am someone who spends most of his life stressing children's capabilities, urging myself and others to see children as whole people, not incomplete incompetents. But face to face with a child in his or her room, with what looks like most of the shelves and cupboards emptied randomly onto the floor, even I have been led to wonder whether some seemingly simple things are beyond

their reach. When you say, 'Take one toy at a time and put it where it goes,' they look amazed and baffled. When you say, 'Take each item of dirty clothing and put it in the dirty washing basket,' they look insulted. When you say, 'Take each item of clean clothing and put it in the drawers we have provided,' they look appalled. If you give them instructions and then leave the room, you discover three hours later that all they have done is put one piece of Lego in a box and since then they've been reading a book called *Impossible Objects*.

Yelling doesn't work. It just paralyses them and they stare at the floor looking profoundly unhappy. Grabbing 'all toys not put away by midday Sunday' and putting them in a large black bin-liner makes them hysterical and (*see* DISCIPLINE) leaves them clinging to your knees in torment – a moment never forgotten for the rest of their damaged lives. There is only one thing left, the oh-so-jolly co-operative method: 'You do that bit and I'll do this bit. This filthy old shirt that you stuffed down the back of the chair goes in the dirty washing basket, doesn't it? Any other takers? OK, first one to put away a hundred bits of Lego gets a prize – ready, steady, GO! Well done, you won. And the prize? You get to do the hoovering. Ooh, I wish I'd won but I'll just have to stand and watch you instead, you lucky thing.'

Yes, of course this might take more effort than if you did all of it yourself, but it's part of the process of teaching them that most of us live our lives without slaves. When I was twelve I went to stay in a French children's camp – a 'colonie de vacances'. We were each given a kind of wooden vegetable box, stood up on end, in which to put our things. We could keep some of our things in our rucksacks too. I don't know what it was, whether it was that up until then my mother had cleared up our room for us, or whether this system of two places to put your things was beyond my conceptual grasp but whatever it was, I couldn't manage it. It was as if I couldn't bear for the rucksack to have no connection whatsoever with the vegetable box. The route between the two was forever strewn with my clothes. Now this 'colonie' wasn't a particularly militaristic set-up but one thing they did bang on about was making beds and sorting your stuff. So every morning the tent monitor would shout at me, 'Range tes affaires, Mike!' and I would think, 'They are ranged, thank you.' But then he would walk all round my bed picking up old shorts and penknives chanting, 'Range tes affaires, Mike!'

A short-lived breakthrough can occur when vital objects are lost or broken. You are sitting quietly one Sunday morning getting depressed by the sheer weight of the Sunday papers when you suddenly hear a ghastly wailing come from a kid's bedroom. 'Oh my God, the wardrobe's fallen on top of him. I told him not to do impressions of mountaineers up the side of it.' You dash in and he is sitting in the middle of the floor, unharmed but sobbing.

'What's the matter, love?' you say, putting your arm round him.

'I can't find the other pulley.'

A nasty, told-you-so little smile creeps on to your face. 'Oh really? Why's that then love?'

'I don't know where I put it.'

'Don't you, love? Perhaps you didn't 'put' it anywhere. Perhaps it just dropped to the floor last time you were using it and it's now in with the football socks and tapes under the bed.'

'Are you laughing?'

'Laughing? Me? Why should I laugh? I haven't got anything to laugh *at*, have I?'

Then at a tactful moment within the next hour or so, you can say, trying very hard not to crow and jeer that one of the payoffs of tidying up is that you can find things. Even little pulleys. Provided you put them in the section marked 'little pulleys'. And here you can prove that you are not being superior and vindictive by showing them how to make little sections on shelves and give them useful labels like 'Best Marbles'. Excursions must be made to Big Red Box shops. More than anything else in the world, children need big red boxes. They are the answer to everything. And when big red boxes aren't available, then small red boxes are good too. There are green trugs with handles and white baskets as well. They are all wonderful and can be labelled and children can be shown how they can fling things into them and suddenly their rooms become magically sorted. In fact, whenever a problem in a child's room starts to emerge, it can nearly always be solved with a big red box. Or several small red boxes. Or a white basket. Or a green trug with a handle.

TV and Video

Ten years ago, the issue preying on people's minds was how to avoid getting into rows over who watches what and whether it's possible to ration children's viewing. Now the situation has completely changed. Most of the children that I meet seem to have TVs – and sometimes VCRs too – in their bedrooms. The adults have finally won back their TV sets, they don't have to ask their children's permission to watch *Blind Date*. If kids don't like what adults watch they can zoom off to their rooms. How different this is to what used to be called Family Viewing, when families huddled together on the three-piece suite and parents acted like film board censors tut-tutting at rude bits, nodding with approval at worthy bits and sending you out when it got beyond the pale. Family Viewing is nearly dead now, except for the rare occasions when families say, 'Let's watch the World Cup together'.

So what is there left to say? If you've given your child a telly, not a lot. Apart from making sure children get their homework done, you can't complain that they're watching too much or the wrong things. I see this as a massive shift in the balance of power between parents and children. Adults other than parents have always had a direct route to children. In Victorian times it was Sunday school teachers. There was a time when it was scout masters, guide leaders and boys' and girls' club leaders. For a time there was the radio and pop records. Now, TV programme makers know that they have a direct line through to children as young as four and five, without any parent censors in the room. Part of the success of people like French and Saunders or Harry Enfield rests on their 'invisible' young audience loving the rudeness and naughtiness of such programmes.

The significance of this is less, are children becoming slaves to the box? Or, are they putty in the hands of advertisers? Or any other doom-laden scenario. Rather, it has put a big whack of autonomy right into young children's hands. They can sit in their rooms, switcher in hand, creating an evening's entertainment out of bits and pieces of programmes and ads that they want to watch. Over the next ten years we will see the advance of the why-should-I? kid. Why should I do what you tell me when I can switch other adults on and off with my switcher? Why should I do the homework you tell me to do, when I can get at information and ideas in my own way on TV? Dangerous stuff, huh? I've seen it happening.

It will have its effect in schools as well. Basically, schools haven't changed much since Roman times. Teacher stands out in front and imparts information to children sitting in front of him or her. It is very inefficient, rarely gets the intended results and has to be heavily supplemented with homework, parental input, and exam panics to get kids on to the next stage. In the future, schools faced with children who have spent years sampling their own entertainment and information, will have to supply more and more learning bays and resource centres, more and more open-ended studies and projects for children to sample their own education too.

Maybe this sounds terribly futuristic. But take a visit into the upper schools of City Technology Colleges and modern private schools and it's already happening. All that has to happen is for it to filter through to mainstream secondary and primary schools. Oh yes, and a few trillion pounds. If it's not spent though, schools will become more and more a battleground between two cultures: the Roman and the sampling.

In the here and now, however, most of us wonder if TV is rotting our children's brains, turning them into psychopaths, or at the very least making them less willing to read books and listen to us. If you really are worried by this, then don't give them a TV in their bedroom. Otherwise you end up having rows over what are contradictory messages: one says 'have all the autonomy you like' and the other says 'oh no you don't, watch what I tell you to.'

My own feeling on the matter is that we waited 'til they were about sixteen before our oldest two got a TV in their bedroom.

Before that time, because we are fortunate to have a kind of play-room, then it was possible to put a children's TV in there that was, if you like, more censorable. We can ration viewing of that TV because it is in a communal space but the family as a whole still has the freedom to watch different things when we want to. It means we can prevent wall-to-wall viewing without invading bedrooms.

I don't think there is much particularly wrong, or, for that mat-ter much particularly right about TV. I happen to watch loads of it. The problem is, firstly, if it's the only leisure activity your chil-dren have and, secondly, they believe everything they see. It fol-lows from the first that you have to help children find other things to do, other things to get interested in. It follows from the second that you have to be prepared to watch your children's programmes, to argue with what you see, state opinions so even if your children disagree with you, they see that television isn't God but merely a form of entertainment devised by human beings with views, foibles and failings like the rest of us.

If we can't be bothered to do either of these things because we are too busy watching TV ourselves then we are hardly in a posi-tion to accuse our children of watching too much. They will spot the hypocrisy before we do. You know the kind of thing: 'Yeah, well, you can't talk.' Nasty but true.

Writing

Even at this moment my children are praying for the day when they will be able to carry about with them a small computer that writes what you say. They will of course eventually each have one of these – they'll look something like a portable phone – and it will print out as they talk. Fifty or even twenty years ago, this would have seemed total dreamland. Now, most children have played around enough on computers to imagine this and the amazing thing is that it could happen in their lifetimes. All this is a roundabout way of saying that when we talk about learning to write, it's an ever-changing thing. My parents learnt to write at school as part of the business of producing millions of clerks who would hand-copy pages of writing and fill in accounts with pen and ink. When I was at school, offices had been taken over by the typewriter, the portable could be taken anywhere and creative writing was thought to be quite important. Now, offices, schools and homes have word processors, scanners, spreadsheets and databases. Less and less pen and paper writing goes on. All my children think writing by hand is a long, laborious, painful and unnecessary activity. There doesn't seem to be very much I can do to convince them otherwise, especially as they see me doing all my writing on a computer.

If you are blessed with children who think writing is a delight, read no further. I am assuming that for more and more parents the situation is like mine. Let me elaborate. Firstly, it seems to shake down by gender. While girls and boys are equally reluctant – perhaps boys slightly more so – the key difference is in what their teachers keep calling 'presentation'. In other words, the girls are neat and the boys are appalling. It has ever been so. On every school report I ever had, teachers said things like: 'He is probably doing quite good work. I don't know because I can't read it.' This went on for years. No amount of handwriting practice, pen changing, paper changing, shoulder massage or finger exercise seemed to make it any better. Somewhere around the age of sixteen it seemed to get more legible and at eighteen it got more consistent. But by then I was writing thousands of words a week in essays and translations for A-levels, followed by a degree.

I notice with my children that by the time they are twelve and thirteen, they are wanting to do their projects and homework on the computer. They are never going to get as much practice at pen and paper writing as I had. Does this matter? At this moment in time, it probably does. Very soon, I guess it won't. We should probably be sending our children on touch-typing courses from the age of about ten onwards. In the meantime, what do I do about the illegible boys and the reluctant but neat girls?

I've figured with the boys that they were taught joined-up writing too early and too quickly. This meant they had to run before they could walk. For whatever reasons, my lot (and for that matter me) didn't have the motor control required to keep up the smooth, consistent, flowing action that joined-up writing requires. Or is it that we didn't have the visual, mental and physical apparatus to see whole words and sentences as flowing movements? It's as if we were stuck on individual letters. But schooling demands us to rush on and make whole joined-up words. If not, we'll fall behind, not be able to write fast enough for exams etc. etc.

As if to prove this, I notice that my boys can *print* letters quite neatly – the problem lies in the joining up. Whatever I say or do they won't spend hours doing handwriting practice and, based on my own experience, I'm not sure it works. I think what they need to do, and I'm experimenting with this at the moment, is to go back to printing the letters – but at speed. I've said to them, when a joining-up movement seems to emerge, let it happen. But don't think you have to join up everything. It seems to be working. Well, put it this way, legibility is winning, which is a start. This approach is no doubt as old as the hills and perhaps I am only reinventing the wheel, but I got the idea from watching one of my neat but reluctant girls. The older one taught herself to write quickly but legibly through printing fast and letting some letters become joined up, then more, then most – but interestingly enough not all. Now she does all her work on the computer.

But how do we deal with the reluctance? It's very hard to disentangle a reluctance to do the slow, motor thing of writing from the reluctance to do the thinking that is required to write some ideas down. Every teacher knows the groan that goes up when an interesting discussion or observation session has to turn into a piece of writing. All the flow and interchange disappears and you are alone with a piece of paper trying to haul things out of your head and put them into slow, dull shapes on the page.

If you are lucky your children will have a teacher who is trying to make writing matter to them. In my day, this was done with the threat of exam failure, teacher disapproval and a low 'position' in class. Each week we were physically placed in class according to how well we had done in the weekly tests. So out of our class of over forty, at least twenty-five of us lived with a constant and physically apparent sense of failure. We never made it into the right-hand side of the classroom. Nowadays, most teachers will try to make writing matter to the child because he or she has got something to say and someone to say it to.

Such teachers will be constantly trying to find ways in which writing is a matter of 'finding an audience'. Put it this way, every kind of writing implies a certain kind of reader. Every kind of writing belongs to a genre, or type, and the moment we start to read we recognize the type of writing and start expecting certain things from it. When I buy a novel, the cover gives off all sorts of messages telling me that is what it is and when I open the first page I don't expect to see a tax demand personally addressed to me, a travel brochure or the Criminal Justice Act (1994). Similarly, when my tax demand arrives I don't expect to find a poem or a football programme. So writing can't escape from having its audience, its readership implied in and around it.

The problem with a lot of the teaching of writing is that it has pretended that the implied audience doesn't exist and that a real audience isn't necessary for children to learn about writing. So every Monday children are asked to write 'Diary'. My children have always hated doing this. In fact it's not a real diary because it's not a private document where they put things they want to remember. It doesn't serve the function of being a special place to put thoughts and memories and notes. But then it doesn't seem to be a place either where you put down thought-out ideas and stories that you would like to share with other people. The only person who gets to see the 'Diary' is the teacher who doesn't react to the content but merely to whether it is spelled correctly and written neatly. This is not communication and for better or worse my children have twigged the falseness of it, and have become hyper-reluctant 'Diary' writers. Writing the diary simply doesn't matter to them.

So, ideally, your child's teacher will be finding a way of making writing matter because your child has found an audience, large or small, who want to read what he or she wants to write. Now because most children are perfectly good at talking to each other, then teachers will want to show children that writing means something different from chat. The reward of writing is that you've got a bit more time to work things out, to change things, to make it sound good, and look good. This doesn't have to be, indeed it shouldn't be, a dull thing to do, but satisfying because it sorts out and articulates your thoughts and other people may admire and enjoy what you write.

So again, ideally, your child's teacher will be trying out a whole range of different kinds of writing for different kinds of audiences. Maybe the children will write a little play and put it on in front of other classes. Maybe they will write letters to various people in the community about facilities or thank-you letters to visitors they have enjoyed listening to. Perhaps they will write poems that can be shared in the class or in assembly. If they do a project then this can be in order to make a presentation for someone or some people that matter to them. When it comes to writing stories, often the best starting point is through drama, story-telling and story-reading, because it is then that the children's heads are full of the imaginative possibilities of fiction. They are in a mood where characters and plots can be played with. Living in the imaginative world sometimes enables them to reimagine for themselves a story with similar characters, similar worlds.

Now, no teacher can make all writing interesting all the time, and no doubt your experience is that there have been plenty of times when your children admit to hating writing. But then, be honest, so do you. How many of us write for pleasure? Write because we want to? And how many of us do it in a room full of people with someone older and cleverer than us standing over us watching? It's a very hard thing that we are asking children to do. So what, if anything, do we do about this at home?

I would say that whatever else we do, we proceed with great caution! If children are getting cheesed off with writing or they are worried and insecure about it, it is incredibly easy to make it worse. I've seen parents setting their children deadly exercises culled from 'Help Your Child With Writing' books. Mostly these books just make parents feel better and children worse. You'd do better with finding out some word games and quiz books that involve writing. There are quiz books with magic pens for example.

Remembering what I said about 'audience', we can keep on the alert for opportunities. The most obvious occasions are letters. We don't have to make this some awful duty where everything has to be spelled correctly and look perfect. We can use it as a time to show children that a little note is sometimes just right. We can explain that people we've been to stay with would really like to hear from our children. It's sometimes a good thing *not* to read the letter so that it becomes something private between the child and granny or whoever.

Another opportunity for home writing is lists and labels. We are very used to doing these ourselves. But if you have a child who is having difficulty with writing, you can get her or him to help you with shopping lists, things to remember before going out, labels on cupboards etc. It's practical and useful writing and they will see that it is their writing that has enabled you to do something. It's writing for a purpose.

Children often say they want to send jokes into magazines, enter competitions, meet famous people and the like. Always, always encourage them to write in. They may get fan club letters in reply, freebies, mentions in the magazines and so on. As they sit down and write these requests and entries, they will really want to make their writing matter. If you casually mention that the immensely overworked people at the magazine will only deign to read what's sent in if it looks OK then you will be amazed at what efforts they will make.

Finally, do they ever see you write? What do you write? What evidence do you, oh role model, provide for them that writing is worthwhile? Perhaps you are forever writing little sketches for the family to perform, poems that you put up on the walls for everyone to enjoy, family histories for everyone to pore over. On the other hand, perhaps you never write at home apart from filling in bills when you curse them all and the fact that you have to sit there doing them. The fact is, not many of us offer our children good evidence that writing is worth the effort. We keep *saying* that it is and how useful it is and the better you are at writing the better job you will have and all that, but what physical proof do we give our children that this is true or, to be more spiritual about it, that writing is a rewarding, creative thing to do?

Your Life

The sickening thing about books like this one is that really they are all about how your life *is* your children. If you dare ever to dismiss them, shout at them, misunderstand them or, even worse, ignore books on how to make them healthy, wealthy and wise, then consider yourself a worm. Secretly, in private, with our best friends, we can admit to sometimes going through a whole half hour without thinking about our children – but don't report us to the NSPCC, will you?

If the newspapers are to be believed, we are becoming a nation of neglecters who leave our children for hours on end to fend for themselves. Whether these are just media-driven scares or whether they reflect the increased hours that people have to work is impossible to say. It would be madness to try laying down some kind of timetable: virtually all parents attempt a balancing act between earning money, spending time with their children, doing something for themselves as a couple and doing something for themselves separately, as individuals. If we are absolutely honest, it's a balancing act that frequently, if not usually, collapses – someone in the unit thinks that his or her needs are not being met. Someone thinks that they're not getting enough attention, someone thinks that they are overburdened with work, someone thinks that they're not having enough time to themselves . . . and so on. It's why millions rely on the support of grandparents, nannies, au pairs, uncles and aunts and so on.

There are two ways in which a life away from the kids can start to matter: 1) 'We aren't doing things together, as adults, away from children' and 2) 'I'm not finding time to pursue something I've wanted to do for myself and myself alone.' I can't claim to have got anywhere near solving either of these. With the first, quite simply and obviously, there have to be things that you both *want* to do together, whether it be watching the TV, building a shed, staring at the sky or going shopping. To make it happen needs help and planning – enter grandparents, au pairs, nannies, brothers, sisters or whoever is willing. Many people do this from almost the first week they have a child. I meet them, with their sun-tanned faces and sexy giggling after a week in Tenerife while granny looked after the kids. Lucky sods. Many other people slide into a rhythm of life where you wake up one day and realize that the only things you do together are as a family and the relationship between you as adults has been squeezed out and left behind. This moment can be a crisis and it's time for emergency action. Outings must be planned, shows booked, slow walks by canals arranged, baby sitters, grannies and nannies hired. On the other hand, I notice that some people don't see it that way at all, and reach a kind of acceptance that that is what family life is like and you can't really try hiving yourself off as a couple. This is clearly not a matter of right and wrong, even though everyone is looking over everyone else's shoulder to see who's got the magic formula. That's why in rows, one of you says, 'Jean and Dave seem to have sorted it out.' And there follows a catalogue of Jean and Dave's achievements in the world of human relationships. Next week, Jean and Dave divorce.

Then the matter is complicated by the second aspect: doing something for yourself as an individual. Is there time for this too? After the week has been divided up into: time earning money, time with the children, time for housework and chores, time with partner, eating, sleeping, going to the toilet and washing, just how many minutes are left for you to write your novel, go to evening classes, keep fit, meet your friends, paint, dream, look at trees, stare into the middle distance, do your family tree, learn plumbing and the rest? This is real what-is-life-for stuff, isn't it? It's in moments on your own that you get to wonder, just what am I doing here? Am I here just in order to bring children into the world and service their needs? If so, what are *they* here for – to grow up and do just the same to the next lot? Or is it in order to make or do something useful to people other than my children? Or is it in order to have a bloody good time as often as possible?

One obvious truth that is said many times: you never find out what you're capable of until you try. For many, there is scarcely the time or the energy left to even try. The dreams about self-development can often simply stay as dreams. For others, it's more complicated: it's as if they haven't got the equipment to try. It takes a certain kind of self-belief, a risk-all, have-a-go attitude to fight for time on your own, and when you've found that, the next problem is to dare to try something that you have no idea whether you're any good at or not. Lucky people find this in their work. For millions of others in paid work or as homeworking parents it's something over there, out of reach, a source of often unarticulated frustration. The only fragment of advice I have for such people is that it may well be that you are someone who really doesn't have the time or energy left at the end of the week to have a go at something for yourself. If so, then it may be some comfort to remind yourself that children get older and provided you haven't worn yourself out by the time they are in their twenties, it's never too late to do That Thing then. On the other hand, it might be that the lack of time and energy is an excuse. It might be that you've told yourself, what's the point of going to that evening class, joining that campaign, going for that walk, I'm no good at it, it's too far, I'm too old or whatever. If you needed an excuse to gather up some energy or the will to have a go at something, then take the words on this page. The rest is negotiation with partner and arranging the baby sitter.